THE DAY COMMODUS KILLED A RHINO

WITNESS TO ANCIENT HISTORY

GREGORY S. ALDRETE, *Series Editor*

THE DAY COMMODUS KILLED A RHINO

Understanding the Roman Games

Jerry Toner

Johns Hopkins University Press
Baltimore

© 2014 Johns Hopkins University Press
All rights reserved. Published 2014
Printed in the United States of America on acid-free paper

2   4   6   8   9   7   5   3   1

Johns Hopkins University Press
2715 North Charles Street
Baltimore, Maryland 21218-4363
www.press.jhu.edu

Library of Congress Cataloging-in-Publication Data

Toner, J. P.
The day Commodus killed a rhino : understanding the
Roman games / Jerry Toner.
pages cm
Includes bibliographical references and index.
ISBN 978-1-4214-1585-7 (hardback : acid-free paper) —
ISBN 978-1-4214-1586-4 (paperback : acid-free paper) —
ISBN 978-1-4214-1587-1 (electronic) 1. Games—Rome—History.
2. Games—Social aspects—Rome—History. 3. Games—Political
aspects—Rome—History. 4. Violence—Social aspects—Rome—
History. 5. Commodus, Emperor of Rome, 161–192.
6. Emperors—Rome—History. 7. Gladiators—Rome—History.
8. Rome—Social life and customs. 9. Rome—Politics and
government. 10. National characteristics, Roman. I. Title.
GV31.T77 2014
796.0937—dc23   2014012493

A catalog record for this book is available from the British Library.

All figures are from Wikimedia.

Special discounts are available for bulk purchases of this book.
For more information, please contact Special Sales at 410-516-6936
or specialsales@press.jhu.edu.

Johns Hopkins University Press uses environmentally friendly book
materials, including recycled text paper that is composed of at least
30 percent post-consumer waste, whenever possible.

CONTENTS

THE DAY COMMODUS KILLED A RHINO

The Rhino Dies

THE EMPEROR COMMODUS wanted to kill a rhinoceros. And he wanted to do it in the Colosseum. His passion for hunting animals was so great that he wanted to shoot a tiger, an elephant, and a hippopotamus as well. So, at the end of AD 192, he put on fourteen days of the most lavish and spectacular games Rome had ever seen. And the emperor himself was to be the star attraction. When news of this became known, people rushed from all over Italy to see what they had never seen or even heard of before: an emperor in the arena. It was said that the emperor's prowess was so great that he never missed when hurling his javelins or firing off arrows from his bow.

Dressed in a long-sleeved white tunic, made of silk interwoven with gold, Commodus began the games by taking the formal greetings of Rome's senators, who were too terrified of him not to attend. Commodus then changed into a robe of pure purple with gold spangled stars, topped with a matching purple cloak. On his head sat a golden crown encrusted with gems from India. In his hand, he held a staff like that of the gods' messenger, Mercury. Recently, the emperor had taken to dressing as Hercules, the man whose heroic actions had seen him turned into a god. So Commodus used to wear a lionskin shawl and carried a club as Hercules had, and countless statues of the emperor in this herculean style were set up throughout Rome. But before he entered the oval arena of the great Colosseum, which the emperors Vespasian and Titus had built more than a century before, the emperor set aside the trappings of Hercules. They were placed on a gilded chair, and he stepped out before the huge crowd of fifty thousand spectators dressed as Mercury, before throwing off all his clothes except for a tunic.

Except he did not simply step out onto the sand as a normal hunter would. A high catwalk had been built, crossing over the entire length of the arena, and it was along this that Commodus strutted before his captivated public. But this was more of a turkey shoot than a hunt. The supporting walls for this structure divided the animals beneath into small herds and, from his vantage point, the emperor could easily pick them off with his bow and his spears. On the first day he warmed up by personally killing a hundred bears. The crowd cheered and applauded each missile as it struck home. It was hot work. Halfway through the emperor grew weary, and taking a cup in the shape of a herculean club, he downed the cold sweet wine it contained in one gulp. "Cheers!" shouted everyone in the crowd.

On later days he continued the carnage. Animals were led up to him or placed before him in nets so that he could shoot them from point-blank range. He even brought down a gentle giraffe with his cruel spears. But the rhino was more problematic. The presence of a rhinoceros was a sure sign of the greatness of the games. Simply getting the animal to Rome had taken a significant logistical effort. They were difficult beasts to control. The emperor Titus had brought one for his games celebrating the opening of the Colosseum in AD 80. Initially the strange animal was just displayed to the crowd, who stared in wonder at its thick hide and twin horns. But when it came to making the beast fight, the rhino was not playing ball. The keepers tried desperately to goad it into getting angry, cracking whips about it, terrified about what would happen to them if the animal failed to perform. At last, the rhino lowered his head and flamed into a terrible rage. It charged out into the arena and tossed a great bull into the air as if it were a dummy. The crowd, which minutes before had been complaining that nothing was happening, gasped in awe.

This had not been the first appearance of a rhino in Rome. Julius Caesar's great adversary, Pompey the Great, had first imported one for his games in 55 BC, although it is unclear whether the rhino in question was a two-horned African rhino or a single-horned Indian one. Both types were sourced by the Romans, with the famous mosaic from Piazza Armerina in Sicily showing an Indian specimen. Nor was Commodus's rhino, whichever type it was, the first in Rome's history to be actually killed for the entertainment of the crowd. The emperor Augustus had one hunted as part of his games in 29 BC to celebrate the opening of his temple to Julius Caesar, his adoptive, dead, and deified father. Roman leaders seem to have had a thing about killing rare breeds. With skin up

Mosaic showing the capture of a rhino

almost two inches thick in places, a rhino is not an animal that is easy to kill even with a modern rifle. We can only imagine at how many arrows and spears, or how much assistance from others, it took before Commodus finally managed to fell the poor beast.

We have an eyewitness account to thank for all these vivid details. Dio Cassius was a senator, as his father had been before him, and he like his peers was forced to attend, salute, and cheer the emperor. Twenty years later when Commodus was long since dead, Dio wrote an eighty-volume history of Rome covering a period of almost 1,500 years. His section on Commodus's reign is full of accounts of the emperor's strange antics. His contempt for him is obvious. He had seen all the emperor's foibles close up.

Dio did not think Commodus was evil by nature. The chronicler thought the emperor extremely guileless. But this simplicity in combination with his cowardice meant that he had fallen into and been led astray by bad company. He soon acquired perverted, cruel, and luxurious habits, all of which fared badly in comparison with his hard-working, modest, and intelligent father, Marcus Aurelius.

Why did Commodus behave like he did? Was he simply mad? The fact that he was just the latest Roman leader to see the merit in importing a rhinoceros for his games already suggests that his actions need to be seen in broader historical context. Commodus himself was also involved in a long-running battle with the senate, which he had come to hate. At the end of his games, Commodus approached the rows of senators and held up an ostrich's head, which he had sliced off at the very top of the neck with a sickle-shaped arrow. He did not speak, but simply shook his head with a grin that made it clear that he would like to do the same to the members of the senate. Dio's response was to start laughing at this ridiculous scene of the world's most powerful man threatening them with an ostrich's head. But laughter was never a wise option when faced with a tyrant, and Dio was forced to chew some laurel leaves from the wreath on his own head in order to conceal his amusement.

Do we take Dio's account at face value? One of the main problems that ancient historians always encounter is that the sources that survive are biased, full of rhetoric, and often plain wrong. Should we treat Dio's eyewitness account as being a true and accurate record of events or were there other issues influencing his text? This short book tries to answer these and a number of other questions that Commodus's odd behavior raises. Why did emperors spend vast resources on lavish spectacles and even want to appear in them? Why did the Romans enjoy watching the slaughter of animals and seeing men fight to the death? How best can we in the modern world understand what was at stake in the Roman games?

The games have always proved a fascinating phenomenon for modern audiences. Mass slaughter, execution, and gladiatorial combat provide a heady cocktail of violence and brutality of a kind that we in the West today thankfully almost never experience (which is sadly not true of many other parts of the world). Not surprisingly, these events provoke strong emotions. The Christian tradition of hostility toward the games also colors our view of what was going on in the arena. It is impossible not to think of the games without thinking of Christian martyrs being thrown to the lions (which, while it did happen, was actually quite rare). It is hard for many to understand how such a great civilizer as Rome could also have developed such a taste for violent public spectacles. One modern writer described these "bloodthirsty human holocausts" as "by far the nastiest blood-sport ever invented." He claimed that "the two most quantitatively destructive institutions in History are Nazism and the Roman Gladiators."[1]

Undeniably horrific as the games appear to a modern outlook, it is equally true that in the Roman world the games represented something both civilized and peculiarly Roman. Seneca argued that the Romans saw the turning of a man into a corpse as a "satisfying spectacle."[2] The amphitheater came to represent, as it still does, the quintessential Roman building. Images of gladiators were also incorporated into a variety of domestic situations: as decorations on lamps, as wind chimes to ward off evil spirits, as splendid mosaics, and as wall paintings. Some wealthy Romans chose to have their villas decorated with scenes of death and execution. The aim of this book is to try to understand the importance of the games within a wider social context and explain the various different attributes that enabled them to play such a role. It is worth remembering that the games also included other popular shows such as the chariot-racing in the Circus Maximus and the frequent performances of the theater. So, while I concentrate on the animal hunts and gladiatorial shows of the arena, I also bring in evidence from these other public spectacles to show how varied a phenomenon were the Roman games.

I would love to be able to step back in time and go to the Colosseum. Not to see the carnage; I doubt I could have coped with it. But to see the hunts, the brutal executions of criminals and the highlight of the gladiators was to see Roman society encapsulated in a single spot. The games have become central to our view of the Roman Empire as having been addicted to decadence. I have tried to give some sense of how much more complex this institution was in reality. The first chapter gives a version of the various entertainments that would have been offered at Commodus's fourteen days of games held just before he died, during which he killed the rhino. It describes the many forms of combat, torture, execution, and martyrdom that such games generally entailed. The chapter also looks at the many other forms of nonviolent spectacle that were in evidence. Theatrical displays, lotteries, gambling, and music all added to the enjoyment. Later chapters will show how the games had political dimensions, being intimately bound up with the nature of an emperor's relationship with the senate and the Roman people; social dimensions, in that the crowd played an active part in the overall performance; and cultural dimensions, because the games drew on deep-rooted strands of meaning for their importance and effect. Just putting them on required a huge logistical effort, which in itself shows just how important they were for the Romans. And the book ends by looking at the games from the point of view of the victims, to try to see how some sought to resist this overwhelming cultural force.

CHAPTER I

Commodus's Great Games

IT TOOK A GREAT DEAL of effort to learn how to kill a rhino. Commodus had employed as his instructors the most skillful Persian bowmen and the most accurate Moroccan javelin throwers. In the end, through a combination of natural talent and hard work, the emperor surpassed them all. In his villa at Lanuvium, about twenty miles from the center of Rome, the emperor had fired thousands of arrows and hurled hundreds of spears at targets both dead and alive. His marksmanship was second to none.

Now the leader of the known world was here displaying his skill in the Colosseum before the massed ranks of the Roman people. As well as the bears and the rhinoceros, he shot deer, roebuck, and horned animals of all kinds. When confronted by docile creatures, he dared to come down from his catwalk to the arena itself to pursue them, anticipating their dashes and killing them with deadly blows. When hunting any kind of more dangerous beast, such as a lion or leopard, he usually stayed out of harm's way on his terrace, although he did transfix an elephant with a pole. His prowess was so great that he almost never needed a second javelin to kill an animal. As soon as an animal jumped up, he would strike it down with a shot to its forehead or its heart, either of which would kill it instantly. When one hundred lions appeared through a trapdoor, as if emerging from the earth itself, the emperor killed them all with exactly one hundred spears. He even timed it so that they fell in neat lines so that the spectators could count them easily.

The crowd marveled at the emperor's skill. They also wondered at the amazing variety of animals that were on show before them. From far-off India and

Mosaic showing a hunter spearing a panther

Ethiopia, from Britain to the north and the German lands beyond the Rhine, came a menagerie of exotic animals. But Commodus was certainly not the first emperor to have created such a zoological fantasy. A century before, for example, Titus had celebrated the Colosseum's opening with battles between cranes and elephants. Nine thousand animals were slain in total in Titus's extravaganza. Even women took part in the killing of them.

Nor was he the last. A decade later, in AD 202, Septimius Severus celebrated his various military victories and his tenth year in power by holding extraordinary spectacles. Sixty wild boars fought together, an elephant was slaughtered, and a new species from India, called the corocotta, never before seen in Rome, was said to have been displayed and then killed. This strange beast had the color of a lioness and tiger combined and broadly resembled them too but also combined the features of a dog and a fox. But the highlight of the show came when the entire bowl of the amphitheater was dressed up to look like a giant boat. Suddenly, the whole scene collapsed and revealed seven hundred different animals. From the debris rushed bears, lions, panthers, ostriches, and bison, all charging about in their confusion. All were picked off by the hunters.[1]

Yes, there was nothing new about the animal cruelty of Commodus's games. It had become common practice to begin the games that took place in the amphitheater with a morning hunt, the *venatio*. Animals were sometimes shot by specialist huntsmen, who, like Commodus, killed the animals with arrows and spears and often used dogs to help them pursue their prey. Or the animals could be made to fight each other, with a bull versus a bear a popular combination. The combatants were driven on by whips and hot irons until one had savaged the other.

But cruelty was not the only option. Some animals were simply displayed to the admiring crowd. Others were decorated to make them even more interesting. Bulls could be painted white, their horns gilded with gold, or sheep could have their fleece dyed scarlet or purple. Or the hunters themselves gave displays of elaborate acrobatics in order to escape the furious charges of the beasts that tried to attack them. Trained animals also gave displays to amuse and entertain the audience. Once a group of lions chased hares before tamely bringing them back and dropping them at their master's feet. It seemed that nature itself had been conquered.

In accordance with tradition, the hunt had started Commodus' games. But much had already happened before the start of the show proper. The night before, as giver of the games, the emperor had given a feast to the gladiators who were due to appear the next day. People were free to come and watch these men have an ancient version of the condemned man's last meal. Some of the gladiators ate heartily, making the most of what might be their last meal and keen to ensure they carbo-loaded for the great exertions of the following day. Others had no appetite at all, terrified at the prospect of what was to come.

On the day of the games itself, the emperor had led a great procession into the arena. The long parade included musicians, the performers themselves, and platforms carrying images of the gods and the deified emperors. The gladiators were dressed in colorful purple cloaks with gold embroidery. They strutted along, followed by slaves who carried their weapons and armor. These heroes of the arena were often well-known to the audience, and lifelike portraits of them had been put up in the public porticoes before the games as part of the advertising for the show.[2] The crowd cheered on their own favorites. After the procession had arrived, a sacrifice was held calling on the gods to continue their divine support for the Roman state.

As Commodus went up to his imperial box, the crowd could settle back in keen anticipation of the extravagant entertainment that awaited them. They knew that every effort would be made to amuse and thrill them. They could hear the muffled bellows of the beasts incarcerated in the cells beneath the sand-covered wooden floor of the arena itself (the word arena comes from the Latin for sand, *harena*). Placards were carried around that told the crowd in what order the events would take place. Those who were illiterate relied on those who could read to tell them what was on the program. Attendants came around handing out free snacks. A fine mist sprinkled the crowd with balsam-scented water. And then, in a lull after the emperor had made his grand appearance as a hunter, came a lottery. Little wooden balls rained down on the crowd. Immediately they started to scramble to get hold of them, and punches and kicks were thrown in the undignified rush to grab one. For these were vouchers, which entitled the lucky holder to swap it for a prize, ranging from cash and food to luxury items like gold, slaves, horses, or even property.

After the hunt, came the executions. It was now approaching midday and the crowd was beginning to thin out as some left their seats to go out for lunch and perhaps a siesta before returning for the gladiators in the afternoon. The entertainment became a bit more down market. A condemned criminal was wheeled out, shaggy-haired, unarmed, and tied upright on a small trolley.[3] He was confronted by a leopard. Normally a docile creature, the cat had been maddened by whips cracking about him. It leapt on to the man's naked chest and grabbed his face between its powerful jaws. He was unable to fight back as his hands were tied behind his back. Blood streamed from the great gashes which the cat's sharp claws and teeth made in his flesh. "Enjoy your shower!" shouted some of the crowd, laughing at the blood raining down around the victim.

No one in the crowd knew for what crime this man had been sentenced to such a fate. He might have been a murderer, a prisoner-of-war, or a runaway slave. These condemned criminals were sometimes armed lightly with wooden weapons. With no training, they had no chance against the animals sent in against them; it just prolonged the agony. Not surprisingly, some preferred to take their own lives rather than face such a fate. One German prisoner went to the toilet and shoved the sponge stick, which Romans used to clean their backsides, down his throat and so choked to death. Another was being taken to the arena in a cart and, pretending to be nodding off to sleep, pushed his head between the spokes in the wheel and so broke his neck.[4]

The executions were not always straightforward. Some were staged, with the condemned becoming the stars of their own destruction. Scenes from history, mythology, and literature were all popular. So one man's arm was held over a fire to represent Mucius Scaevola, the legendary hero of early republican Rome who had thrust his hand into a fire to prove to the enemy how brave

Roman soldiers could be. The mythical castration of Atys was reproduced, as was the living pyre of Hercules on Mount Oeta. Even the mythological union between Pasiphae and the bull became a reality. These were executions that had been turned into dramatic statements of society's desire to punish those who broke its laws.

The venue for these gruesome midday executions was not some grubby prison or public space. The Romans had spent increasingly large amounts on erecting phenomenally grand buildings to house such festivals of death. This had culminated in the Colosseum, which sat in the heart of Rome. Architecturally, it represented a series of triumphal arches, reflecting the victories over the Jews that had paid for its construction. It was decorated with all manner of opulence. Statues, stucco decoration, and brightly colored plasterwork all greeted the spectators as they arrived. The whole experience was carefully designed to generate a feeling of total sensory overload. From the emperor's gold-braided purple toga to the blaring horns of the musicians and the scents of the water sprinkled on the crowd, this was an intensely physical experience for all involved. The spectators rose as Commodus led the procession into the arena and chanted his name in ritual acclamation. The trumpets sounded to start the contests. Later, flutes signaled the first gladiatorial fight. These sensory markers punctuated the performance and told the audience when to do what. They acted as triggers to tell the crowd what was about to happen and how to feel.

All of the drab mundaneness of ordinary life was overturned in these great imperial games. Light and color were used to dramatize events. If we are to take our somewhat exaggerated sources at face value, the emperor Domitian had a circle of lights lowered into the amphitheater at dusk and so turned night into day. Caligula held nighttime performances and lit up the whole city, which was itself taken by many as a sign of his unnatural tastes. Caligula and Nero even favored colored dusts—either white, red, or greenish-blue copper colored—instead of sand. In summer, sailcloth awnings were unfurled over the crowd to shield them from the harsh sun. In the theaters, these awnings were sometimes made of colored silk to create the special effect of irradiating the crowd and stage with different colors, in the manner of stained glass. This shade was also symbolic of the life of leisure that had traditionally been the preserve of the landed gentry. The shade of the crowd combined with the glittering reflectivity of the sand to spotlight the action taking place in the center of the auditorium. The best fights were thought to be those where the combatants did not run away into the corners but where the butchery was done in the middle where all in the amphitheater could see it clearly.

Exotic animals, with their appearance sometimes enhanced by decoration, their roars and the cries of the victims all pandered to the people's taste for extravagant and over-the-top entertainment. The spectacles were in every way truly spectacular. Not many of the audience would have have been able to appreciate or even understand every nuance contained in the elaborate decoration, the inscriptions, and the mythological references. Instead it was the broad brushstrokes of exaggerated performance that appealed to them. The details of the setting collectively served to create an ambiance where the crowd could feel that the whole world was simply a resource for its own entertainment. This was the ultimate in leisured luxury.

By this time it was afternoon and the B-rate executions had been completed. The empty seats had filled up in expectation of the day's highlight. Bring on the gladiators, they cried. Paraded around the arena before the crowd and then presented to the emperor himself, the fighters were what the people had really come to see. But the crowd would be kept waiting a little longer. First there was a bloodless warm-up act between fighters with wooden weapons and whips, just to get the crowd in the mood. Then there was a formal test of the gladiators' weapons to show that they were sharp enough to kill a man. At some contests there may have been lots drawn to see which pair would fight first, although it was probably more usual to have them arranged to maximize the excitement, with the fights culminating in the headline bout between the two biggest stars. Then the horns sounded and the contests began.

What was it like to be a gladiator? How did it feel to face death in front of fifty thousand baying Romans? One fictional account that survives from the Roman Empire describes the thoughts that went through a novice gladiator's head as he waited to go out into the arena. He describes how the whole place was buzzing with the preparations for death: one man was sharpening a sword and another was heating the metal plates in a fire, plates that were used to check that a fallen gladiator was not pretending to be dead. Knowing that he stood no chance against his experienced opponent, the novice saw stretchers being dragged in that would later carry out his body. All about were preparations for his own funeral. Then the trumpets blared "with the fatal sound portending my death."[5]

Then there were wounds, groans, and gore everywhere. His terror was palpable: "the totality of my peril lay before my eyes." He started to have flashbacks to happier times as, at the point of death, "the sad remembrances of past pleasures came to mind." He was overcome with despair that he is "doomed to die an ignominious death." Such despair was thought to be characteristic of a gladiator's mind.

When you look at how scantily clad these gladiators were, it is easy to understand such feelings of hopelessness. Dressed in a loincloth tied by a belt and protected only by a helmet and shield, leather straps on the legs, and an arm protector, their torsos were left bare and open to attack. There were variations on the dress and weaponry according to the type of gladiator. The *retiarius*, the netfighter, carried a trident and a weighted net in which to ensnare his opponent. Shieldless and with his head bare, he was protected only by a shoulder guard on his left arm, which often had a raised metal lip to protect the shoulder and neck. He also carried a long dagger in the same hand as his trident as a weapon of last resort. Lacking armor, he needed to fight from a distance, probing and prodding with his trident and trying to trip and entangle his opponent with his net. Of course the price for armored protection was a loss of mobility. The more heavily armored gladiators, such as the *murmillo* (named after the type of fish that decorated his helmet), against whom the *retiarius* usually fought, lacked the speed and agility of the nimble netman. So too did the Thracian, who carried a smaller shield but wore longer shin guards called greaves to give added protection.

There were other more exotic types. The *essedarius* fought from a chariot British style and may have been introduced by Julius Caesar after his campaign in that island. The *laquearii* hunted their opponents with lassos. Others fought with two swords, one in each hand, and one type, the *andabata*, even seems to have fought blindfolded. Nor did they always fight alone. Sometimes groups fought against each other, re-creating famous battle scenes from Rome's glorious military past. Even naval battles could be staged by using specially constructed lakes near the Tiber, in which as many as three thousand men fought.

We should not get too hung up on the exact details of different gladiators. There seems to have been lots of local variations among different kinds of fighters. There were no fixed pairings or order of fights. Minor alterations between shows were probably appreciated as variations on a well-known theme. What mattered most was generating a good contest. Although very different in style and appearance, great care was taken to match the level of skill between opponents in order to maximize the excitement. Nobody wanted to see a walkover. Even the gladiators thought it beneath them to have to fight an inferior, because they knew they would get no respect for beating a worthless opponent.[6]

Let us imagine that at Commodus's games, the first fight was between the common pairing of a netfighter, the *retiarius*, and a pursuer, called a *secutor*. Their names were those of mythological pretty boys, Narcissus and Hyacinthus.

There is no direct evidence for betting on gladiatorial combats, but it seems highly likely that it did take place (although the chariot racing in the Circus Maximus was probably the more usual focus for gambling). This can only have added to the crowd's interest. The *secutor* was a novice and pushed forward at the *retiarius,* jabbing with his short sword and peering out over the edge of his shield. The more experienced netman danced backward, watching and waiting for an opportunity to thrust the harpoon at his opponent's head or legs or to swing his net over him. Despite the cooler feel of a December day in Rome, which did not see the temperature rise much above 13 degrees Celsius or 55 Fahrenheit, it was hot work. The pursuer, lugging around his heavy armor and weaponry soon began to puff heavily. His helmet served only to constrict his breathing further.

Unencumbered by such restrictions, the netman hopped about, happy to wear down his opponent in a war of attrition. The referee and his assistant and the men's trainers urged the pair to pick up the pace when they showed signs of flagging. The background noise made it almost impossible for the *secutor* to hear what they were saying from within his heavy helmet. The fight had a musical accompaniment, with flutes, horns, a water organ, and even singing ringing out across the arena, and sometimes the music even seemed to be in time with the action of the fight. The crowd urged on their favorite gladiator, shouting out suggestions. Perhaps the *secutor* heard one because he suddenly managed to catch the netman's side by pretending to go one way but swiftly thrusting the other. "He's got him!" shouted the crowd.

The blood ran down the netman's leg but this was only a superficial flesh wound. He had been trained to put up with such minor difficulties. Furious at himself for having lost focus he quickly regained his composure and escaped the pursuer's frantic attempts to finish him off. These exertions were to prove costly to the *secutor.* As he grew more tired, gaps started to open up in his defense. The netman started to play with him as his lunges became increasingly desperate. The crowd loved it and cheered him on as if he were a matador toying with an exhausted bull. His greater experience—he had fought eight contests before, winning six of them and being spared in the others—was beginning to tell. Then, once he felt he had entertained the crowd enough, the netman closed in for the kill.

The tired *secutor* was too slow in pulling back from a weary thrust. This gave the netman the chance he needed. Deftly wrapping the net around the *secutor*'s sword arm, he knocked away his opponent's shield with his trident and pulled him down to the ground. Standing over his opponent, the *retiarius* pinned him to the ground with his trident pressed against his neck. A gladiator knew he had to fight until he saw the finger. Here it came. The prostrate *secutor* let go of his sword and raised the index finger of his left hand. He was asking for mercy.

It was Commodus, as giver of the games, whose decision it was whether to let this wretch live or die. But it was his duty to listen first to what the crowd thought. As the emperor surveyed the ranks of Romans before him the noise grew to a crescendo. Some cries of "Let him go" could be heard. But they were drowned out by others of "Kill him!" Almost everyone seemed to be jabbing their thumbs, although it is not now known for certain whether it was upward or downward for death or deliverance. The *secutor* must have known his fate before Commodus signaled it. Now it was time for him to die like a gladiator.

The victor removed the fallen gladiator's helmet. The *secutor* then grasped hold of his conqueror's leg and held back his head in a way that exposed his neck. A deathly hush took hold of the arena. Fifty thousand Romans stared intently at this murderous ritual taking place before them. The *retiarius* had laid down his harpoon and now gripped only his long dagger, which he raised slowly into position, making sure to place it accurately on his victim's throat. The first time he had had to kill a defeated opponent his hand had wobbled dreadfully, despite all his training. The loser kept his eyes fixed straight ahead, showing no inkling of emotion. After a short pause, the netman pushed the knife down through the man's jugular and into his heart. He made no mistake. The gladiator died almost instantly.

Many in the audience cheered, others looked intently at the dying gladiator's face. Attendants dressed as Mercury ran over from the side to take the body away, but first one of them touched his bare arm with a red hot poker just to check that he was really dead. There was little doubt this time. Sometimes, though, gladiators could appear to be lifeless but were in fact trying to escape their fate. Or they were simply mortally wounded. These would be taken out and finished off either by having their throat cut or by having their head smashed in with a mallet by an official dressed as Charon, the ferryman to the underworld. Other attendants came over to where the death ritual had been acted out and raked over the sand to make sure there was a clean slate for the next bout.

The winner took it all. The cheers, the applause, the glory, and the cash all went to him. And he received a palm branch to wave to his admiring audience as he soaked up their adulation in a lap of honor. The cash prize had been stipulated in his prefight contract. Commodus's father, Marcus Aurelius, had attempted to limit the size of these rewards to between 20 and 25 percent of the gladiator's purchase price but with little success. Now the gladiator went up to the emperor's official and was given his victory purse gold coin by gold coin. The crowd counted out each one as he took it: "One! Two! Three! . . ."

It would not have been surprising if Commodus felt a bit jealous of all this adulation. The arena certainly created a place where even the emperor had to compete for the people's affections. Whether he was driven by this kind of envy is impossible to say, but Commodus did not only appear in his games as a hunter of rhinos. That day, as the highlight of the festivities, the emperor himself was to descend into the arena and fight in combat. The day Commodus killed a rhino was also to be the day he fought as a gladiator.

This was not the first time he had faced an opponent in a staged battle. It was said that Commodus engaged in gladiatorial bouts seven hundred and fifty or even a thousand times, but most of these took place in private behind closed doors. For years he had practiced as a gladiator on his country estate. He even had a room in the largest of the gladiator training centers. Sometimes, he would swish his sword so close to his opponents that he looked like he was trying to give them a haircut. Other times, he deliberately sliced off the tips of their noses or their ears. He killed a man occasionally. Most of his crowns and titles he won by beating *retiarii*, since he himself liked to appear as a *secutor*. Commodus was so proud of himself that he accepted the honors usually given to real gladiators and took as much pleasure from them as if he had been awarded a triumph for a great military victory. By the time of his great games of AD 192, he seemed to be casting aside all restraint and was promising to kill all kinds of wild animals with his own hands and to take on the very bravest of gladiators.

Commodus was prepared to fight publicly even though gladiators were socially and legally inferior to the average citizen, let alone the emperor. He seems to have had a few qualms about this when he first started to practice privately at being a gladiator. He would cover his bare shoulders with a purple cloth in some kind of display of false modesty. But he also made sure that everything he did in his fights was reported in the city gazette, the daily record of significant events in Rome, so he hardly seems to have been trying to keep it a secret.

Physically speaking, Commodus was vigorous enough for such exploits. But he was not the perfect specimen so often portrayed in his imperial statues. He is said to have had a conspicuous growth on his groin, which people could see through his silken robes. People used to write comic verses alluding to this deformity, although none of these survive. But there was no such joking when Commodus was actually there. When the emperor was due to enter the arena as a gladiator all of Rome's senators and knights had to attend, including Dio Cassius. One brave man, Claudius Pompeianus, refused to appear, but made sure to send his sons in his place. He could not bear to see the son of the great Marcus Aurelius behave in so debased a fashion. But the rest of Rome's elite dutifully turned up and shouted out whatever they were told to. They had to repeat the chant, "Commodus, You're the boss, You're number one, You're the luckiest man alive! You are the champion!"

Some of the ordinary people stayed away. They had heard a rumor that Commodus planned to shoot a few of the spectators as well all these exotic animals, in imitation of one of Hercules' labors in which he killed the Stymphalian birds. It might sound unreasonable that people would have believed such a far-fetched story, but it was known that the emperor had once brought together all the men in Rome who had lost their feet as a result of disease or accident, and then, after tying imitation snakes round their knees and making them hold fake stones made of sponge, clubbed them to death, pretending that they were the giants of Greek mythology killed by Hercules.

But most were too keen to see their emperor appear as a gladiator, and the stands were full. On the first day, he had personally come down to the arena and chosen which gladiators should fight each other. Now the emperor himself was going to fight in public as one of them. Proud of his left-handedness, and having recovered from all of his hunting exertions over lunch, Commodus strode out onto the sand to face a professional opponent. Thus far we are reminded of the conclusion of Ridley Scott's film, *Gladiator*, where Commodus faces the disgraced general Maximus and is finally brought to an appropriately gruesome end. In real life, Commodus had no intention of exposing himself to such needless danger. He was armed with a wooden sword and his opponent carried only a stick. The gladiator had also been hand-picked by the emperor himself to ensure that he could be relied upon not to get too carried away. Beside him as he fought stood his trusted lieutenants, Aemilius Laetus, the prefect, and Eclectus, his valet. This was riskless fighting. Everyone knew what they had to do. After a few vigorous exchanges made under the watchful eyes of the emperor's guards, the gladiator fell down and begged for mercy. The crowd roared their approval at their leader's prowess, who mercifully spared his opponent from death. He then kissed his companions through his helmet.

All of his opponents knew what was good for them and let him win easily. In return they suffered nothing worse than a few blows with a wooden sword. In a private contest, a gladiator called Lefty had once rejected the emperor's offer of a dagger with a dulled point and told him that he would fight him unarmed. Commodus immediately feared that his opponent planned to wrest his own dagger from him and assassinate him and so had him put to death. But Commodus himself seemed to believe that he won his fights through talent alone. When he had finished, he returned to his imperial box and watched the rest of the combats. There was no child's play now. Iron was swapped for wood, and great numbers of gladiators were killed. The emperor actually insisted on death at one point when a group of victorious fighters hesitated to slaughter their defeated opponents. Commodus ordered that they all be tied together and made to fight each other, with the result that many died.

Commodus charged the Roman state a million sesterces as an appearance fee—a sum that would have made a normal man eligible to become a senator—a fee he felt suitable for an imperial gladiator. After these great games, he appears to have become even more extreme in his passion for gladiatorial combat. He no longer wanted to live in the imperial palace but intended to move into the barracks at the gladiatorial school. He ordered that he should no longer be called Hercules, as he had previously ordered but instead by the name of a famous gladiator. He arranged for himself to be awarded the title of "Captain of the Secutores." Some of his behavior seems megalomaniac. He removed the head of the huge statue to the sun god which Nero had first put up—the Colossus from which the Colosseum drew its name—and replaced it with his own head. On the base of the statue he did not have inscribed the usual imperial titles but simply this: "the Conqueror of a Thousand Gladiators."

Commodus was the only emperor in Roman history to have appeared as a gladiator in public shows. Others practiced the moves in private. Some actually fought in private. Only Nero had gone so far as to appear in public in various theatrical performances and in the chariot racing at the Olympic games (an event in which the judges wisely awarded him the gold medal even though he fell off). It was an act that our eyewitness to these events, the historian Dio Cassius, thought shocking for a man of Commodus's rank. Dio accepted that the emperor's hunting of animals succeeded in winning the approval of the crowd for his courage and his marksmanship. But he thought that when Commodus came near naked into the amphitheater, waving wooden weapons, and pretending to fight as a gladiator, then he presented a disgraceful spectacle. A Roman noble whose emperor father had won real victories on the battlefield instead of mock fights in Rome should not have been shaming his high position with such disgusting exhibitionism. Why then did he do it? What was a stake when Commodus shot the rhino and then debased himself farther by fighting as a gladiator?

CHAPTER II

When in Commodiana

COMMODUS HAD THE SAME birthday as Caligula (August 31). He was quite touchy about this. He once had a man thrown to the wild beasts just because he had been seen reading a biography of Caligula. This might suggest that Commodus was well aware that negative opinions about him existed and that he knew what senators like Dio Cassius thought of him. The emperor was also, no doubt, anxious that he would meet a similar fate to that of his predecessor, who had been assassinated in a coup. But is it really fair to see Commodus's activities in the arena, as both hunter and gladiator, in the same light that upper-class writers like Dio did? To answer that question we need to look at the political context in which Commodus's seemingly bizarre actions took place.

To anyone who has read the main ancient accounts of Commodus's reign, it is immediately clear how indebted we are to Dio. This is hardly surprising. Dio had lived through it and had experienced the emperor's threats firsthand. He had had to chew his laurel leaves to stop himself disrespecting the emperor by laughing at his antics. This proximity meant that Dio was able to spice up his account of the life of Commodus with all kinds of weird details about the emperor's personality and behavior.

But Dio himself had reservations about including these stories. He was nervous that this was not the stuff of real history. His eighty-volume history of Rome was not a light read intended for a mass audience. This was a weighty tome to be read by other literary gentlemen like himself. It focused on the great military and political events that had shaped the capital of the great empire. Commodus decapitating ostriches was not really what it was meant to be about.

Dio felt obliged to excuse himself for including this material. "In case anyone thinks I am sullying the dignity of history by recording these events," he writes, "these things were done by the emperor himself and I myself took part in everything seen, heard and spoken." So he says that he has included even the most trivial events as if they were really very important. It is because he has experienced them directly that he is able to describe them with such accuracy and detail. No one, he says, has a better knowledge of these events than he.

This all sounds reasonable enough. But are we right to believe Dio's account? Should we accept his argument that because he lived through Commodus's reign then he has greater claim to accuracy and the truth? Or is Dio's account as full of biases and rhetoric as any other ancient account? Did Dio have a vested interest in portraying Commodus as he did?

Commodus was the first emperor to be "born in the purple," meaning that his father had been emperor at the time of his birth. He could trace his ancestry through five generations of emperors. There were rumors that he was not really the son of Marcus Aurelius but the illegitimate offspring of an affair between his mother, Faustina, and a gladiator. It was said that when Marcus had heard of his wife's passion for this gladiator he had him killed and then she had to bathe in the blood of her dead lover before sleeping with her husband. It was said to have cured her infatuation, but their son Commodus was born a gladiator in spirit. The contemporary Fronto said that, as a boy, Commodus actually looked very much like his father. It seems that story about his possible parentage was just another tall tale invented to fit the fact that Commodus later took an interest in fighting as a gladiator.

His twin brother died at the age of four, leaving Commodus as the heir to the throne. His philosophy-loving father had taken great pains with his son's education, employing a long line of distinguished teachers to train him in the liberal arts. The emperor was sufficiently pleased with his son's progress that he appointed him co-Augustus at the age of fifteen. Three years later, he succeeded his father as emperor after Marcus Aurelius had died on campaign in what is now Vienna. Coming after a long series of successful emperors who had attained their position by being adopted by the previous incumbent on account of their personal merits, Commodus's accession was not universally greeted. Dio described the accession as the descent "from a kingdom of gold to one of rust and iron." Gibbon saw in Commodus's reign nothing less than the start of the long decline and fall of the Roman Empire.

Another account of his reign, the "Life of Commodus" in the *Lives of the Later Caesars*, paints a lurid picture of the emperor's early tendency toward degeneracy and vice. It claims that, even in his earliest years, he was degraded and shameless, cruel and lewd, foul-mouthed and debauched. He excelled in things that a future emperor should have thought beneath him, such as drinking, dancing, singing, and even whistling, as well as playing the fool and pretending to be a gladiator. The account gives one story that it says gave ample warning of what was to come. When Commodus was twelve, he went to the baths and found the water too cool. So he ordered the bathkeeper to be thrown alive into the furnace that heated the water. Thankfully, and bravely, the slave who had been ordered to do this put a sheepskin in the furnace so that the smell of burning permeated the baths and fooled Commodus into thinking that the punishment had been carried out. But this life of Commodus was written probably two hundred years after the emperor's death. It is full of exaggerated tales that fantasize about imperial excess and depravity. We should be very careful about taking it at face value.

The same source tells us that in his teens Commodus was supervised by a group of teachers and mentors who had been handpicked by his father. He hated them. He did everything he could to avoid their influence and showed no regard for decency. He spent money like water. He gambled, womanized, pimped, and even lived like a gladiator. The stories sound unrealistic, the kind of standard, made-up stories an ancient author would say about someone he was trying to put down. It is tempting to see Commodus's reaction against these paternally appointed overseers as nothing more than a youthful attempt to assert himself and his own personality and to stop himself from being seen as his father's puppet.

Marcus Aurelius had spent most of Commodus's youth away on campaign. It is also tempting to think that, left to grow up in a palace surrounded by sycophants, Commodus lacked the fatherly hugs that might otherwise have made him better adjusted. But Commodus's upbringing was hardly different from that of many wealthy Romans at that time. His education was provided by specialists in the liberal and military arts. And, in Dio's contemporary account, we find no sense that Commodus was already corrupted as a youth. In fact Dio believed he was a simple and gullible young man, whose vices were only to reveal themselves once he had become emperor. Many of the most extreme stories come from much later sources who seem to have invented them to sex up their tales of an emperor who by then had acquired a dreadful reputation.

Later writers seem incredulous that a man with so high a reputation as Marcus Aurelius could not have seen his son for what he was: an egotistical, neurotic maniac. But the evidence suggests strongly that Marcus Aurelius planned carefully for his son to succeed him. His promotion to co-ruler does not smack of a man trying to keep his heir out of power. Nor did his making him a consul at the age of only fifteen, the youngest in Rome's entire history to that point. He made a point of celebrating with Commodus joint triumphs for successful military campaigns. In AD 178 Marcus hastily chose a wife for his son, before heading off on campaign. Her name was Crispina and she came from a powerful consular family, precisely the kind of intra-elite marriage that suited an heir to the throne. Commodus was taken on some of these campaigns in order to educate him in the arts of warfare and to introduce him to what would eventually be his main power base: the army. On his visit to the Danube frontier, Marcus even had Commodus give out a cash bonus to ensure the legions' loyalty to the dynasty. Marcus could have adopted another man as co-Augustus and passed over his son. He did not. Everything points to his wanting Commodus to succeed him when he died.

Dio's hostility to Commodus is revealed in his description of Marcus's death. He reports suspicions about the cause of his death, claiming that Marcus had died, not because of the (unknown) disease from which he was suffering, but because his doctors wanted to do Commodus a favor. Dio was not present at the deathbed, although he does say that he was told this clearly by unknown sources. If you were one of the doctors treating an ailing emperor, would you have colluded with your colleagues to kill a respected ruler of almost twenty years' standing? Would you have risked everything out of a vague notion of helping out his heir? How could you have even been sure that his son would have seen his father's murder as a favor? Of course, this portrayal of events is possible, which is why it was easy for Dio to peddle these rumors. When Dio was writing his history, Commodus was long since dead. He knew the kind of ruler he wanted to portray Commodus as having been. And being an indirect regicide was a good start to the process of assassinating Commodus's character.

Marcus had been a stern, stoical man, far tougher on himself than most people are. The fact that Commodus had a more relaxed attitude to life should not in itself be seen as a sign of his immorality and ineptitude. Although only nineteen when he acceded to power, he did have some experience from his position as co-emperor and from being on campaign. It is certainly true to say that Commodus does not appear to have had much interest in imperial administration. Happy to leave such dull and tedious matters to a few trusted henchmen, he preferred to devote his attention to the games.

Above all, Commodus showed no interest in continuing Marcus's protracted campaigns against the tribes north of the Danube. After his father's death,

Commodus called a halt to the fighting and returned to Rome where he was met with great joy. The whole senate came out to greet him, a fact that Dio conveniently omits to mention despite being a senator at the time. The new emperor then celebrated a triumph and doled out cash benefits to the citizens. It all boded well for the new reign.

For those of the Roman elite who hoped to have a chance to win glory for themselves on campaign, Commodus's decision to sue for peace was reprehensible. For many older senators, it may also have seemed like a betrayal of his father's wishes and a diminution of Rome's power. But it made a lot of sense. Marcus's campaigns had been hugely costly and, with the empire suffering from a serious plague that probably came back from earlier campaigns in Persia, manpower was in short supply. The legions had been at war for years, and both sides seem to have found it easy to reach a settlement. More important, the peace lasted. The border remained stable for another seventy years. This was not some weak surrender that simply stored up trouble for the future.

Commodus had no real rivals at this time. But antagonism between him and the senate was high. His father had treated this ancient and venerable institution with great respect, and the senators had grown used to this imperial flattery. But Commodus was younger and more independent. He knew his power stemmed from the army and the Roman people, and it was these two power bases he sought to cultivate, not what he saw as the desiccated traditionalists in the senate who always compared him negatively with his father.

This conflict was to culminate in an attempt to assassinate Commodus at the end of AD 182 or early 183. While Commodus was in the amphitheater, he was attacked by a relative, Claudius Pompeianus, who strode purposely up to the emperor brandishing a sword and uttering the words, "The senate sends you this dagger." But this all took so long that Commodus was able to escape. Many others were implicated in the plot. Later sources suggest this fiasco was primarily an internal family matter, with his eldest sister, Lucilla, being portrayed as its main driver. She was exiled and later killed, but her children were spared. Whether Pompeianus was actually revealing the truth about the assassination attempt—that it had been planned with widespread senatorial support—is impossible to say. But it would hardly be surprising if Commodus had taken his words at face value.

Commodus faced a series of plots during his reign. It is hard for us to imagine what it must have been like living life under this sword of Damocles. It would not be surprising if the effect on Commodus was to make him feel vulnerable and adopt a more dictatorial attitude toward his enemies. He would certainly not have been the first or last Roman emperor to have reacted in this way to the anxiety of holding imperial office. Filled with fear and unable to trust those around him, Commodus largely withdrew from public affairs. It was what Rome's second emperor, Tiberius, had done a century and a half before, when he retreated to his villa on the isle of Capri.

Like Tiberius, the effect of such a withdrawal was to create gossip about what the emperor was really up to. Emperors were so central to the political and upper-class social life of Rome that their absence left a void that came to be filled with stories about them. Rumor-mongering of this kind need not have mattered, but it allowed Commodus's opponents a chance to tell all kinds of exaggerated tales, a habit that later writers either drew upon for their source material or simply continued. So we find stories that "reveal" how wantonly cruel Commodus was: that he cut a fat man down the stomach so that his intestines fell out. Or how oversexed he was: that he kept a man as a kind of pet, who had a penis that was larger than that of most animals, before appointing him to the priesthood of Hercules. Or how crazy he was: that he often mixed human excrement with the most expensive foods and would then taste it to shock his guests. And how power mad: that he ordered the praetor Julianus to dance naked in front of him and his mistresses while clashing cymbals and making funny faces.

Was Commodus really that bad? We have seen that his change in military policy toward a more defensive strategy was in many ways sensible. In Scotland, similarly, he abandoned the northerly Antonine wall in favor of the more easily defensible Hadrian's wall. These shifts in military policy also had the effect of stabilizing the empire's finances after the ruinous expenditure on war by his father. By relying on financially astute deputies, such as the Praetorian prefect, Perennis, expenditure was reduced. Cash handouts to the citizenry remained at a stable level as did army pay. Nor were taxes raised apart from on the wealthiest. This was achieved despite the fact that the empire continued to face the problems associated with the plague. The benefits of peace for the provincials in the Danubian provinces need hardly be stated. Commodus also seems to have listened to the complaints of unjust treatment from rural tenants, agreeing to the demands for justice of the farmers of one imperial estate in North Africa that was known as the *saltus burunitanus*.

Commodus also acted more leniently toward the Christians than his predecessors did. It is alleged that his wife, Crispina, had been caught in adultery, and, after she had been first exiled and then killed, Commodus's new favorite was a woman called Marcia. Her parents were freed slaves and she was a Christian. Under her influence, Commodus reversed his father's aggressive policy toward this minority sect. The plague that had occurred in Marcus's time created a general shortage of manpower in the empire and had forced him to recruit gladiators for the army. The ensuing shortage of gladiators led to an increase in the cost of holding games, a phenomenon that the emperor had tried to limit by fixing prices. Another of Marcus's responses was to persecute Christians to increase the supply of condemned criminals (or martyrs as the Christians saw them) to the games. In the same act, Marcus also found in the Christians a suitable group to act as scapegoats for the problems of the plague. Nero had provided a precedent for this when he had blamed the Christians for causing the great fire of Rome in 64 AD. Commodus ended all these measures and also freed those Christians whom Marcus had condemned to the mines of Sardinia.

Commodus was certainly hostile to the senate. He dismissed those who had been close to his father and took delight in insulting many senators by making them perform degrading tasks or by giving them offices far below their station. He had no senators in his group of close advisers, although he did award consulships to several eminent families. In part we can see this as a continuation of the second century's trend toward more powerful and centralized imperial authority. Emperors were to become steadily more dictatorial and authoritarian over the next two hundred years, and Commodus was merely part of this process of change in the power structure. Relying on powerful right-hand men who owed their position and their loyalty directly to the emperor himself can be seen as part of this transformation in how emperors operated. It reflected the fact that the senate, for all its prestige, no longer mattered.

Commodus was also undoubtedly a populist. And just as it is clear that he was reviled by most senators, the evidence also suggests that Commodus remained popular with both the army and the Roman people throughout his reign. Providing and appearing in the games played a central role in maintaining that positive relationship. His coins, for example, emphasize the great generosity Commodus displayed toward the common man and the ordinary soldier. Many of his inscriptions reverse the usual ordering of SPQR (*Senatus Populusque Romanus*, "the Senate and the Roman People") to PSQR (*Populus Senatusque Romanus*, "the People and the Roman Senate"). One of the principal ways in which he funded such largess to the army and the people was to tax wealthy senators. It is not surprising, therefore, that they gave him a bad press in the same way that they had similar emperors, such as Nero, before him.

But despite the various plus points for the early years of Commodus's reign, it is the final two years that seem to have cemented his reputation as a mad, bad emperor. First, he increasingly tried to present himself as the demigod Hercules. His megalomania went so far that he renamed Rome, its people, and even the entire calendar in his own honor. His oppressive regime toward the senatorial elite intensified. And, perhaps worst of all, he appeared in public as a gladiator and hunter in the arena, legally inferior entertainers, and so cheapening the office of emperor in the eyes of his detractors.

Passing yourself off as Hercules might to us seem strong evidence of Commodus's insanity. But ancient rulers as far back as Alexander the Great had tried to publicize links between themselves and this hard-working god. Trajan and Antoninus Pius, emperors close in time to Commodus, had also advertised their close connection with Hercules, both of whom are usually classified as "good" emperors. Nor was Commodus the last, with Diocletian, for example, linking his tetrarchy to the labors of Hercules. Commodus differed only in that he openly declared himself to be Hercules's latest incarnation.

Hercules was a very popular divinity, especially in the army and among the general population. This was a down-to-earth Olympian who had earned his divinity through his own labors. He also had an all-too-human side, being caught drunk, driven mad, or womanizing depending on which versions of the myth you read. His image was widespread and found frequently in baths, as the patron god of hot springs and the gym. He was also the divine symbol of effort and energy. There were clearly many positive attributes with which an emperor might want to align himself. And from AD 183 numerous coins show Commodus and Hercules, together with the god's trademark club and lionskin. The final two years of Commodus's rule saw an intensification of the use of this image. Perhaps he was seeking greater protection from his divine mentor? Whatever the motivation, it led to an increase in Commodus's training as a hunter, as he tried to hone the skills so that they would so impress the Romans at the Colosseum that people would think him a god reborn.

Hercules seems to have been the last in a long line of gods that Commodus linked himself with during his reign. Previously, he had entered the arena dressed as Mercury, a god whose speed and versatility meant that gladiators themselves often adopted his name as a stage name. He is said to have practiced Isis worship and even have gone so far as to have shaved his head as her followers often did. He got so carried away that he is supposed to have once forced some devotees of the goddess to beat their breasts with pinecones until they were nearly dead. Commodus may also have been interested in Mithraism. He was the first emperor to adopt the mithraic title of *invictus*, "the undefeated one." If the emperor had been an adherent of this religion—in which authority

Bust of Commodus as Hercules

was drawn directly from the god Mithra—he could have found in it support for the stronger form of imperial power that he seemed to be trying to establish.

With the adoption of Hercules as his alter ego, Commodus seemed to have been saying to his Roman audience that he was a man, who had, by carrying out the will of the gods, not only brought peace, order, and prosperity to his subjects, but had himself become a demigod. His senatorial critics put it down to Commodus's unhealthy obsession with the games. But it might have been the other way around: that he was driven to become a peerless hunter and gladiator in order to emulate his hero and to prove that he had himself attained divine status. Did he believe he was a god? It is impossible to say and the question is probably misguided. The classical world always had a more permeable notion of the border between the earthly and the divine. It was not in itself a sign of insanity to believe that a human could become divine: many emperors were deified after their deaths once it had been ratified by the senate. Perhaps all that Commodus was guilty of was not waiting for posthumous senatorial approval and for pursuing a novel avenue for achieving that divinity.

Commodus's attempts to refound Rome after over 900 years of glorious history are harder not to see as indications of advancing isolation and megalomania. The catalyst for this was probably the great fire that swept Rome in AD 191. He might have got the idea from Mithraic mythology, which saw humanity as attaining true peace and prosperity after a great conflagration. Whatever the source, Commodus saw this as an opportunity to start afresh. He decided to reinvent Rome. No wonder many people subsequently blamed him for starting the fire in the first place, in the same way that they had blamed Nero for starting the fire of AD 64, when he took advantage of its aftermath to build his Golden Palace. Even though Dio describes how Commodus came to Rome in order to encourage those trying to control the fire, the fact that he then gave himself the title "Founder," *Conditor*, as part of a package of reforms designed to herald a new Golden Age, meant that many people thought him guilty of arson to aid his plans.

Commodus changed his own name as part of this rebirth. He became Aelius Aurelius Commodus dropping the names Marcus and Antoninus as a way of distancing himself from his Antonine ancestry. His full title had twelve names, and the months of the year were renamed after them in his honor: August, named in honor of the first and greatest emperor Augustus, was changed to, what else, Commodus. Next came Hercules for September. For October Invincible (*Invictus*), for November All-Conquering (*Exsuperatorius*), and for December Amazonius, after his mistress Marcia, whom he loved to have portrayed as an Amazon and for whose sake he is said to have wanted to appear in the arena dressed as an Amazon. These measures came into effect from July, sorry, Aurelius, AD 192.

It went on. His palace became the Domus Palatina Commodiana, "the Commodian Palace," the legions *commodianiae*, and the senate was restyled Senatus Commodianus. Dio must have loved that. And in the greatest act of hubris, Rome itself became Colonia Lucia Annia Commodiana, "the Colony of Commodus," or Commodiana for short. For all Dio's doubtless hostility, the senate passed the resolution without a murmur and for good measure it awarded Commodus the name Hercules and pronounced him a god.

Commodus used to send pompous messages to the senate such as, "The Emperor Caesar Lucius Aelius Aurelius Commodus Augustus Pius Felix Sarmaticus Germanicus Maximus Britannicus, Pacifier of the Whole Earth, Invincible, the Roman Hercules, Pontifex Maximus, Holder of the Tribunician Authority for the eighteenth time, Imperator for the eighth time, Consul for the seventh time, Father of his Country, sends greetings to the consuls, praetors, tribunes, and the fortunate Commodian senate." We can imagine Dio and his colleagues exchanging smirks with each other as this was read out. Vast numbers of statues were erected representing him as Hercules, and it was at this point that Nero's Colossus was remodeled in the emperor's likeness. The senate voted that Commodus's new era should be officially called a "Golden Age."

There also seems to have been an intensification of the dictatorial style. Dio records how Commodus began to act in an increasingly arbitrary and authoritarian way. On one occasion this "Golden One," this "Hercules," this "god," as Dio mockingly calls him, suddenly drove into Rome one afternoon from his estate and held thirty chariot races in the space of two hours. He brought random accusations against wealthy individuals in order, Dio believed, to claim their assets because he was spending too much money on extravagant games and on his lavish lifestyle.

Then came the ostrich. Holding up the bird's severed head, as that other demigod Perseus had done with the Gorgon's head, in front of the rows of senators at the games, he raised his bloody sword in his other hand. The senate got the message. They all started to think their days were numbered. Their fears were justified in that Commodus was executing all kinds of high-ranking Romans, from his own family members, to six former consuls and their families, to current consuls and proconsuls, and innumerable others. The nobility understandably believed, or perhaps just hoped, that the Great Fire was an act of divine vengeance for this tyrannical behavior.

His stupendous games featuring his own star-billing proved to Dio that Commodus had completely lost the plot. The games at the end of 192 were by no means the first he had given to ensure popular support. But this was the first time that he had been the main participant and attraction. For Dio it was inconceivable that a Roman of such high rank should willingly disgrace himself in that way. Gladiators, like other performers in the games, were legally inferior beings, being subject to legal *infamia*. Now Commodus seemed to identify himself ever more closely with this group of outcasts. Starting in AD 190, he cut his hair short in the gladiatorial fashion. At his games he received the formal greeting of the senators while dressed as a gladiator.

Was Commodus trying to show that he was above all the normal rules of behavior, that he could do what he liked? Or was trying to curry favor with the populace who he worried might have abandoned him after the recent fire? We are told that his appearances were very popular. So, it seems clear that he was trying to gain legitimacy by appealing to the people in an innovative and direct way. That he was doing so outside the traditional avenues was itself unlikely to appeal to a conservative like Dio. By bringing the senators into the performance both during the greeting and by threatening them with an ostrich head, Commodus was also appealing to the people's antipathy toward the wealthy and powerful. They took great delight in seeing these high officials being ridiculed for their entertainment. The senators themselves became part of the popular spectacle. It also showed just how all-powerful the emperor was.

Senators like Dio saw this behavior as evidence for Commodus's advanced madness. But the show was not put on for them—it was put on for the people. Dio struggled to conceal his laughter as he watched Commodus wave an ostrich head at him. Was this a small act of resistance to the oppressive regime? Was it a release of nervous tension? It is worth remembering that, as he held the bird's head, Commodus was also grinning at them with a kind of rictus, baring his teeth like a dog. He seems to have enjoyed making the venerable senators sweat in front of the crowd. Perhaps he was making a comparison between the flightless bird, which sticks its head in the sand at the first sign of danger, and the useless old institution of the senate. If so, was he suggesting that it was ripe for destruction and that no one would miss it if it met such a fate?

On a later day in the AD 192 games, Commodus summoned the senate to the amphitheater to see him fight again as a gladiator. But this time he raised their spirits because he ordered them to wear woolen cloaks, something that would only normally be done when an emperor had died. Then on the last day, Commodus's helmet was carried out through the gates from which the bodies of dead gladiators were normally dragged out. If he was hoping merely to mourn the ending of the games or intimidate the senators with images of death, it backfired. Dio tells us that these events caused absolutely every one of the senators present to believe that they were surely about to be rid of him.

And so it proved. It was said that Commodus had planned to march from his room in the gladiators' barracks on New Year's Day dressed as Hercules, accompanied by other gladiators, and, in an ultimate display of godlike power, murder both the consuls and take their place himself alone. The prospect was considered so outrageous by those closest to him that, fearing for their own lives, they had him assassinated the day before he was to take office. His mistress Marcia first poisoned him, but he was unaffected, so the wrestler Narcissus was sent in to strangle him. It was in some ways an appropriate end for a gladiatorial god.

The senatorial backlash against the regime was swift and harsh. In the first session of the senate held after Commodus's death, it was decreed that his memory should be officially erased from record. His statues were thrown down, the Commodian calendar was torn up, and Rome became Rome again. The senate's decree was vitriolic and mocked him with the kinds of chants used in the games: "Let the murderer of citizens be dragged in the dust. . . . Let the statues of the gladiator be overthrown. Let the memory of the murderer and the gladiator be completely erased. . . . Throw the gladiator into the incinerator. Listen to this Caesar: let the murderer be dragged off with the hook." Commodus was now nothing more than a dead, worthless gladiator whose corpse was being taken off for an ignominious burial.

The senate replaced their statue of Commodus with one of freedom. His weapons were sold off, including some studded with jewels. But their celebrations were to be short-lived. Imperial Rome in the late second century was not a place where freedom flourished. Once Septimius Severus had established himself on the throne, after the chaotic Year of the Five Emperors, Commodus's rehabilitation soon started. Eager to establish links between himself and the previous Antonine regime, Severus criticized the senate for its hypocrisy in its attacks on Commodus. "Do none of you fight as gladiators?" he asked, and "Why have some of you bought his shields and those golden helmets of his?" Commodus's body was transferred to Hadrian's mausoleum, now the Castel Sant'Angelo on the banks of the river Tiber. Within three years, Commodus had been restored to full honor.

How are we to judge Commodus's reign? Recent scholarship has tried to perform a comparable rehabilitation to that which Severus did. Was Commodus simply a popular favorite who, like modern Hollywood producers, understood and played up to the tastes and demands of the average citizen? Is his bad reputation simply the effect of a character assassination carried out on him by the literary elite of the senate? Or was he a paranoid tyrant? The truth is that we can never reach any final conclusion to these questions. But asking them does make us go back to the sources and realize how limited we are by them. Even Dio was writing almost twenty years after the events which he witnessed had taken place. He was living under a new regime and was keen to distance himself from the excesses of a previous emperor. By casting Commodus as a ridiculous figure, Dio was implicitly pledging his allegiance to the new imperial power. And he wants to emphasize that he was not taken in by the fictions of the old regime.

One of the main points of Dio's story of the ostrich was to show that Commodus lacked the sense of humor of a good emperor. Emperors should know when to make and take a joke, especially in the games when their character was most clearly on display. The games were a place where imperial generosity was paramount, and that extended to allowing his subjects a certain freedom of expression. Terrifying them into chewing leaves because they were too afraid to laugh did not reveal any such spirit. Commodus's actions might, in his eyes, have underlined how powerful he was and how he had no need of the senate. But the senate represented the traditional elite within Roman society, and cutting them off excluded a powerful part of the Roman order from his government. By concentrating on the army and the people, Commodus left his rule lacking the authority and stability that senatorial support might have brought. And in terms of his legacy, he needed the senate to give him the write-up he no doubt felt he deserved.

The Colosseum has always provided an image of Roman grandeur and decadence combined. It would be nice to think that Commodus was killed by a man of such true republican virtues as Maximus in the film *Gladiator*, who sought to rid Rome of corruption and then return, like General Washington, to his farmstead. The reality was far more complex. By appearing as a hunter and a gladiator in the games, Commodus sought to establish a new, direct relationship between himself and his people to the exclusion of traditional interests. He chose to do this at the games because they had always been closely bound up with an emperor's relationship with his people. Games sat at the heart of the imperial political process. We cannot know every motivation that Commodus had in appearing as he did, or whether he was in some ways mad. But by looking at the wider historical and political context of the games, we can understand something of why he chose the arena to play out his personal fantasies.

CHAPTER III

An Emperor Loves His People

COMMODUS MAY HAVE BEEN a populist but he was not always popular. In AD 189 the plague broke out again, with senator and historian Dio reporting that two thousand a day were dying in Rome itself. That winter Rome was also hit by food shortages. People began to demonstrate against Commodus's right-hand man at the time, a Phrygian named Cleander, who they blamed for having bought up most of the grain supply and putting it in storage for his own ends. A former slave who had grown up in the imperial household with Commodus, Cleander was thought to have wanted to become emperor. To achieve this end, people said he planned to get control of the people by hoarding their food and then to win over the army by making a generous distribution of grain.

Shows at the Circus Maximus were one of the rare times that ordinary citizens could make their feelings known to the emperor. People began to complain openly about Cleander as they congregated at the Circus for a day's racing. When the seventh race was about to start, a crowd of children ran out onto the track, led by a tall, grim-faced young woman who many subsequently thought must have been a goddess. The children shouted in unison, complaining about the people's dire situation. The crowd then joined in and started to bellow out all kinds of insults about Cleander. In the end, many jumped down on the track as well and set out to confront Commodus who was away in his palace. Cleander sent some troops out against them and killed or wounded a few but this did not deter the rest. They pressed on determinedly until they had managed to get close to the emperor. The crowd does not seem to have been hostile to the emperor himself, for Dio records that people were still wishing blessings upon him. But they wanted Commodus to hear their complaints about Cleander.

So far Commodus had not been told what was going on, but with the crowd now so near he had to be informed. He was terrified—Dio delights in telling us that he was the greatest coward—and he at once gave the people what they wanted: Cleander's head. The emperor ordered that his loyal henchman be executed along with his son, who was being brought up in the imperial household. The boy's head was smashed on the ground. The crowd snatched up Cleander's body, defiled it, and stuck his head on a pole, which they carried around the city as a trophy. Commodus claimed that he had been deliberately kept in the dark so as to absolve himself from any blame. How could anyone believe that an emperor so devoted to his people could treat them in such a way? He also distributed benefits to the people to underscore his affection for them.

One of the notable features of this account is that complaints about Cleander began in the games. There was a simple reason for this. Rome had long since ceased to have any genuine form of representative democracy. The turmoil and succession of conflicts during the late republic—when dominant warlords like Julius Caesar, Pompey, Mark Anthony and Octavian had carved up the state between them—had ultimately seen the end of the traditional system of popular assemblies. This was a development that denied the Roman people a formal voice in high politics, even though it can be argued that such a voice was always fairly marginal and largely under elite control. The ultimate winner of this power struggle, Octavian, later restyled as Augustus, faced a problem of how to get the Roman people to buy in to his new system of imperial rule. The games provided a major part of the solution.

The games had always offered an avenue for elite competition as wealthy politicians sought to outdo each other in attracting popular political support. Julius Caesar had once gathered together so many gladiators for a show that the senate had rushed through a law to limit the number of fighters that anyone could keep in Rome.[1] It was like having a private army to entertain the people that could easily be turned militarily against the state itself. By the time of Commodus the empire was an autocracy, but the games offered a way for the emperor to retain popular support and also allowed a means for direct communication between himself and his people. The games therefore filled a need for two-way communication and became symbolic of the reciprocal relationship that had been established between ruler and ruled. As such, it is important to emphasize that the spectacles were not just fun. They met an urgent need to establish a new political settlement between the Romans and their leader after the troubles of the late republic. In some ways, this dialogue can be thought of as teaching the emperor how to do his job. It was when acting out his role as supreme patron to his people that he truly felt what it was to be emperor: giving generous gifts, hearing his people's complaints, bullying aristocrats, granting clemency to the fallen, all of these were acts that graphically brought home the reality of imperial power to everyone. Getting actively involved in the shows and fighting as a gladiator as Commodus had done simply served to express this relationship in its ultimate form.

Why did Romans think that the games provided a suitable place for such political expression? We would think it strange if people today voiced complaints about issues such as food supply, war, and maladministration during a football game. One of the reasons for the popularity of the games was the high value that the Romans placed on leisure. In Latin the word for leisure, *otium*, came first in the conceptual order ahead of its opposite, work, which was termed "not-leisure," *negotium*. One writer claimed in a letter that the Roman people were concerned above all with two things—the grain supply and the games— but that they cared most about the games.[2] This would seem counterintuitive to us. We would imagine that people would worry more about food than entertainment. The author of this, Fronto, was a member of the wealthy upper classes, and he might have gotten it wrong. But most emperors seem to have believed that games were at least as important as grain, and they spent liberally on both. Having money to enjoy expensive entertainments was what characterized the rich. Ordinary Romans were keen to share in this leisured lifestyle, and the games were the means by which they did so.

A culture of benefaction existed. The elite saw it as their duty to give gifts and benefits to the Roman people. In return the people gave their political leadership support. In part, this culture existed because the elite needed the support of the masses. Rome was a city of a million inhabitants by the time of the empire—an enormous number for a preindustrial city—and such a potentially volatile and hostile crowd always had the potential to threaten emperors as they had Commodus in response to Cleander. But there was also a more purely cultural side to this benefaction. A hard-wired belief existed in all Romans that there was something remarkable about the Roman people. Here was a citizen body who had provided manpower for the legions that had conquered the known world and beyond. They deserved to share in the fruits of that empire.

These rewards were the same kind of benefits that accrued to a wealthy landowner—the perks of a leisurely life of wealth. There was a sure supply of food, which came to the citizens of Rome in the form of a grain subsidy. And then there was the entertainment in the form of the games. The two benefits, which Juvenal famously called "bread and circuses" were inextricably linked. Giving people bread meant that the amount of work they had to do to put food before their families was reduced. It freed up time for leisure. Rough calculations suggest that a family of four received about 40 percent of the cost of their basic food requirements each year in state handouts. That did not represent the total cost of living, as they needed to pay for other essentials like housing and clothing. But food did represent a much higher portion of average household expenditure in the ancient world, so it is clear that the grain supplied by the state gave a significant boost to the average Roman citizen's available income and allowed them to spend time at the entertainments that were given to them in parallel.

Giving the Roman people the spectacles they deserved and receiving their political support in return served to justify and legitimate imperial rule. That is why emperors made so much of their generosity in games giving. It really mattered to them to demonstrate how many shows they had put on because this acted as an index of the legitimacy and popularity of their rule. The first emperor, Augustus, set out a record of his achievements on two bronze pillars in front of his mausoleum in Rome. The text lists in detail the many occasions on which he held games, detailing the huge numbers of gladiators and animals that participated. "Three times," he says, "I gave shows of gladiators under my name and five times under the name of my sons and grandsons; in these shows about 10,000 men fought." He put on spectacles of athletes gathered from all over the empire. No fewer than twenty-six times did Augustus hold animal hunts and in them about 3,500 beasts were killed. He even gave the people a spectacle of a naval battle in a specially constructed lake that measured 1,800 feet long and 1,200 wide, in which thirty warships and many smaller craft fought among themselves.[3]

The games were a big part of any emperor's public relations. The size of Augustus's games almost seems quite modest in comparison with the extravagance of later emperors. His eight gladiatorial shows with ten thousand fighters averages at a respectable 1,250 per show, while his twenty-six hunts killed only 135 animals each. By comparison, a century later the emperor Trajan held 123 days of games to celebrate his conquest of Dacia, modern Romania, in which ten thousand gladiators fought and eleven thousand animals were slain.

The games symbolized the harmony that the emperors liked to believe characterized their rule. Augustus decreed that in the amphitheater the crowd must be stratified according to social status. This seating plan itself became a symbol of the order he had restored to Roman society after the chaos of the late republic. The crowd was expected to play their part in formally backing this new form of stable government by loudly voicing their support through ritual acclamations and chants. There was a payback for gifts of such generosity.

The games played such a big role in imperial ideology that the emperors guarded the right to give them jealously. During the republic, any private family who had the money could put on a show to further their political aims. Augustus limited the power to hold games to a narrow group of close family and officials who had been appointed with his support. He also restricted the numbers of gladiators who could fight to 120. After the emperor Domitian in the late first century AD, the right to give games was limited to the emperor himself or to his representative.

There are many examples of the political use of the games to deliver specific messages in the manner that Commodus seems to have done. The building of the Colosseum on the site of Nero's Golden Palace made a clear statement that Nero's eventual successor, Vespasian, after the mess of the year of the four emperors in AD 69, was a man who put public pleasure before the private needs of an emperor. Vespasian's son Titus also paraded some of the informers who had supported Nero's rule as part of his celebrations to open the Colosseum. The message was clear to all: the old Julio-Claudian dynasty may have been founded by the great Augustus but it had ended up with Nero. A new start was required that returned to the social harmony that had characterized Augustus's reign. The Flavians were the family to deliver it.

That does not mean that everyone approved of the games. Many of the senatorial and literary elite seem to have been dismissive of these popular pastimes and to have treated them as a poor substitute for real political activity. They also often seem to have been jealous of the games for being so popular. The life of leisure, in their eyes, was something that could best be entrusted to the educated and wealthy and not to the common masses. Biased sources, like that of Dio, showed little sympathy with Commodus's attempt to share the sporting interests of the people, in the same way that writers had been so disdainful of Nero's appearances in the theater and the Olympic games. As we have seen with Commodus, this hostility could have serious implications for an emperor's reputation and legacy, because these elite authors were the men who wrote histories. An emperor had to be careful to balance his pandering to popular tastes with showing sufficient respect to upper-class traditions. But whatever qualms they may have had, the elite were compelled to turn up and support the emperor at his games. Ironically, the very grandees who sniffily thought the games were too appealing to the lower classes were those most prominently in attendance.

Huge imperial games like those of Commodus were rare occurrences. We need to be careful not to start thinking that in a culture where the games featured so powerfully it was somehow normal for an emperor to start shooting rhinos. Games of this magnitude were extremely rare, which is why our sources make such a big thing of them. They were spectacles that were so above the run-of-the-mill entertainments that they deserved to be recorded for posterity. Personal appearances by emperors were even rarer. We have seen that only Commodus appeared as a gladiator and only Nero on the stage and as a charioteer, even though many others played at these sports in private. But in their very rarity, these extreme examples of the fascination that the games had for the Romans serve to tell us how ingrained the games became in the political culture of the wider Roman Empire. Local politics modeled itself on the mutually beneficial relationship between the emperor and his people. Looking at small-scale provincial games can let us dig a bit deeper into the motivations of the local hot shots who spent substantial sums hosting their own more modest shows.

A surviving Roman novel, the *Satyricon* by Petronius, gives us a mocking description of what these unsophisticated, backwater games were like. Or rather, he tells us what a superb spectacle should include and so spells out what was characteristic of a really bad set of games. A great show should have free man fighting, not just a troupe of professional gladiators, presumably because the professionals lacked the zest and energy of self-motivated fighters. Cheap gladiators, it tells us, will not put up much of a fight, no matter how much the crowd shouts at them to get stuck in. There should be lots of different events, one after the other, and they should be real, not just staged. The swords must be good quality to make sure that the fights are done properly. The gladiators must be brave enough that they do not just run away and try to take cover on the edges of the arena. The butchery must be done in the middle for all to see. And the giver of the games should make sure that he takes time to collect lots of different kinds of performer: clowns, women fighting from chariots, acrobats. All of this will, of course, cost.

And it is clear that many local officials went to great effort and expense to put on exciting games, even though these were minuscule in comparison with the great imperial shows. The reason they paid up so readily was because giving games brought popularity and prestige. The games offered clear opportunities for self-advancement and provided local elites with an outlet for competitive display between themselves. It was also a way for them to declare publicly their loyalty to the culture of the dominant Roman regime. The thunderous applause the giver of a show received meant an enormous amount to the host. Cicero rejoiced when he received "wonderful cheers without any hostile catcalls."[4] Putting on games was certainly not simply a voluntary act of generosity on the part of the donors. Roman society expected the wealthy and powerful to provide public benefits out of their own pockets. The games were a status tax, one that local elites throughout the empire willingly paid.

This mutual expectation can be seen clearly in images such as the Magerius Mosaic from North Africa, which commemorates the show put on by a local magistrate in the early third century AD. The mosaic tells the dramatic story of how Magerius stepped forward and volunteered to pay for the cost of providing four leopards, how the crowd chanted his name in return, and how he reveled in this glory.

Magerius owned a fine villa in what is now the small village of Smirat in Tunisia, and he had his splendid mosaic laid in one of the reception rooms. The shape of the mosaic makes it likely that it was intended for the dining room, so that dinner guests could recline on couches on the edges and gaze on the mosaic as Magerius entertained them. The deaths of the four leopards are shown in detail, the spears causing blood to pour out onto the sand. It is striking that it was considered desirable to have a scene of bloody animal destruction as a center piece for domestic entertainment. We would think it strange to see death scenes decorating our dining room walls . The dinner guests became the viewers of Magerius's games, looking on the fights that he paid for.

The inscription in the center of the mosaic describes the moment when a herald came forward after the four leopards had been killed and asked who would pay the five hundred denarii apiece that they had cost. This was probably an elaborately staged request, as it is unlikely that the suppliers of the animals would have had them killed speculatively, in the hope that a local patron would volunteer to foot the bill. Instead, in a preplanned moment of high drama, Magerius ostentatiously stepped forward to announce that he was going to pay, and not only that but that he would pay double what the herald was asking for: a thousand for each leopard. The crowd went wild, shouting his name out loud. "This is wealth, this is power!" they exclaimed. The thrill was so great that Magerius decided to immortalize the moment by having a hugely expensive mosaic made in his home. How often his poor wife must have heard the story recounted to their guests as they sat having dinner around the scene.

Self-aggrandizing mosaics such as these acted as permanent reminders of private munificence and reflected the glory that local elites felt accrued to them from giving games. It was like having a photo of you meeting the president or the queen in a gold-plated frame on the wall. They did not think it was a waste of money to spend so much on giving games or on commemorating them because that was what you did if you were important. The very fact of being in a position to give games showed that you had made it in local society. Most were given by rich holders of public office. What Magerius has the crowd chant in his mosaic reflects what he would have wanted to hear: that he had been generous, had put on a great set of games, and had gained in prestige as a result. That was what wealth and power allowed you to do.

This sense of reveling in the public display of power that giving games allowed the host to feel can also be seen in the many mosaics that feature the decision moment in gladiatorial combats. When one gladiator had fought to the finger and raised it in a call for mercy, we have seen that it was not the crowd who decided his fate but the giver of the games. It was he who signaled whether the loser had fought sufficiently well to be allowed to live to fight again or whether he should be ritually killed. In happier moments, it was the host who could choose to set free a gladiator by awarding him a wooden sword as a symbolic token of his release from service.

A wise host did not decide alone. He listened to the crowd to hear their views. Given that the games had been put on to entertain them, it made sense to give weight to the spectators' wishes. This ritual served as a dramatic metaphor for the Roman political system. The wealthy and powerful acted in the interests of the people, not their own pockets, and they listened to what the people wanted. In return the crowd gave them honor and respect. We can see this clearly in the Symmachus mosaic, which shows two gladiators, called Habilis and Maternus, fighting in a show paid for by Symmachus. But the commentary describes how it was Symmachus himself who "thrust the sword." That did not mean that he personally came down to the arena and killed the defeated gladiator who was pleading for mercy. Rather it was his decision that gave him agency. "I kill him," the inscription states. The crowd responded by saying that they have seen this clearly. "Symmachus," they add, "you are a lucky man!"

But the games were not simply a place for the host to show off his power. He also had to show that he was one of the people. In part he achieved this by paying attention to the crowd's wishes. But he also had to be seen to share their interests and, above all, share their sense of humor. It was this ability to take a joke at his own expense that is a remarkable feature of many accounts of emperors at the games.

Marcus Aurelius, a stern, sober and philosophical man, sat through performances at the theater where a comedian in the performance made jokes about the emperor's wife's alleged lover, Tertullus. The character of the Fool asked the character of the Slave what was the name of his wife's lover. The Slave said it was a man called "Tullus." The Fool asked twice more and on the third occasion, the slave said, "I've told you three times (in Latin Ter) Tullus is his name." Poor Marcus had to sit there and put up with it.[5] The way an emperor responded to such jibes was thought to reveal a lot about his character. It acted as a simple public index of how good an emperor he was. It showed that he understood that he was ruling citizens not just slaves.

The notion that ultimately it was the Roman people who held sovereignty persisted long after this had ceased to have any real meaning. Emperors were therefore keen to show that they were taking their games seriously. For one thing, they were expected to attend. Tiberius attracted a great deal of flak for staying in his villa in Capri during the games and for sending a representative in his place. And if emperors did attend, they were meant to take an active interest. People complained because the serious-minded Marcus Aurelius sat in the imperial box answering petitions instead of following the action. No matter that he was being a hard-working, dutiful emperor. What mattered in the games was that emperor showed openly that he was enjoying the fun as much as anyone. Communicating this fact was not always easy because of the size of the crowd. There was no public address system to announce the emperor's thoughts. His gestures were very important in this regard since they were easily visible and understood. Sensible emperors also made sure that they gave out information on placards that could be read by those who were literate in the audience and the information passed on by word of mouth.

Claudius did this better than any other emperor. He communicated with the crowd informally, made jokes, joined in the counting out of the prize money. He even called the spectators "lords." The emperor Trajan improved his public image by being seen to share the enjoyments of "all Romans." Likewise, the emperor Titus openly displayed the fact that he was a fan of the Thracian gladiators and exchanged banter about it with the crowd through both words and gestures. To underline his man-of-the-people image, he even sometimes bathed in the public baths alongside the ordinary citizens. It is possible to see Nero's and Commodus's actual participation in the games as performers as simply an extreme expression of this kind of direct contact between the emperor and the people.

Clearly there was an element of what one modern commentator has called "unctuous pandering" going on here. But regardless of how sincere emperors like Claudius were being in calling the crowd his "masters," the obligation still existed for them to show that they believed in keeping the people entertained. The provision of games and food to the Roman people sat at the heart of the postrepublican political settlement. It is no coincidence that the Colosseum and the Circus Maximus sat next to the Imperial Palaces.

Rome was almost unique among preindustrial monarchies in having this kind of politicized leisure. The games provided a place where popular feelings could be openly expressed. They were well-suited to this purpose. It was possible for shouts and collective chants to be heard by the emperor. Most important, these opinions were cloaked in the protective cover of anonymity. Criticizing emperors is a dangerous business. Nor did these opinions have to be given in a verbal manner. Simple applause or hissing was enough to make the collective will apparent. The crowd seem to have been most active at the Circus and the theaters rather than in the Colosseum.[6] This most likely reflected the fact that there was a better cross-social mix at these venues, compared with the arena where the audience was weighted toward the top end of society.

Some of the surviving examples of crowd complaint are overtly political. A few years after Commodus's death, Dio was attending the chariot racing at the Circus. He describes how the people made clear their displeasure at the continuing war going on between the emperor Septimius Severus and his rival Albinus. "How long will we have to put up with this?" they shouted. Or a century later, when the emperor Maxentius was being challenged by Constantine for the throne, the crowd shouted out in one voice at the Circus, "Constantine the invincible!" making their political allegiance clear.[7]

Roman politicians were acutely sensitive to these verbal opinion polls. They listened closely to the gradations of applause that greeted them and the complaints that were made against them. The perception that the Roman people needed to be heard meant that many protests were successful. The emperor Titus made sure that he always treated the people with indulgence during the games.[8] He once at a gladiatorial combat declared that he would give the people what they wanted not because he thought it was a good idea but because *they* did. It was said that he never refused anything and he even urged the crowd to ask him for whatever they wished.

The crowd could certainly be very persuasive. Dio records how Claudius was once forced to swear that he was telling the truth in the face of popular doubts about the veracity of his public statements. It was generally believed that his wife, Messalina, was having an affair with the famous actor Mnester. When the actor failed to appear on the stage at a particular performance, Claudius was compelled to apologize for his absence and was forced to swear that he was not being kept at the imperial palace by Messalina. In the end, though, the crowd did not push the matter. They were upset that the emperor seemed genuinely to have no idea of what was going on under his nose, but they also did not want to get Mnester into trouble. The crowd loved his acting as much as Messalina loved his looks. So they kept quiet and took Claudius at his word.[9]

Not all emperors enjoyed this crowd pressure. At one show in the theater, Tiberius had been forced by popular demand to free a certain slave actor. His response was simply to stop going to the games.[10] Nor did emperors always give the crowd what they wanted. The emperor Hadrian was once attending a gladiatorial show when the crowd began to insist on some matter or other (what exactly was not thought worth recording), but Hadrian refused to give in. He sent out a herald to command the crowd to be silent. This was a high-handed action because it was what the autocratic and unpopular Domitian had done a generation before. Fortunately for Hadrian, the quick-thinking herald simply gestured to the spectators that they should be quiet and, once they had complied, said, "That's what the emperor wants." Hadrian was actually so grateful to the herald for not carrying out his rash order that he rewarded him generously.[11]

Not surprisingly, politicians tried to manage the crowd in order to exercise some control of what could otherwise be a volatile situation. Cicero describes how during the republic people would hire a sort of professional cheering squad to try to start chants and to hurl abuse against political opponents.[12] Nero used planted supporters to lead the crowd's cheering when he was on stage. Being a spectator at one of Nero's performances became a tricky matter.[13] Eager to win a theatrical competition on his own merits, the emperor reputedly played the harp but did not sit down when he tired, wiping the sweat from his brow with his own clothes, spitting and snorting all the while. When he finally finished, he knelt and saluted the audience. Then he awaited the judges' verdict with feigned anxiety. The crowd made the theater ring with their enthusiastic applause. They clapped so hard their hands hurt. What else could they do? Soldiers hit them to keep them applauding if they stopped. Some were too scared to leave their seats and were said to have sat for so long that they suffered seizures. Even staying away was a risky option. Informers in the audience made lists of who was absent. They even scrutinized the spectators' faces to look for any small sign of disgust at Nero's antics. The future emperor Vespasian got into trouble for dozing off during one of the emperor's interminable appearances. It was said that it was only his greater destiny that allowed him to survive.

The crowd's inability to express its true feelings was itself a sign that Nero was a substandard emperor. We find similarly dictatorial behavior from the other usual suspects of the abuse of imperial power. Commodus had betrayed these traits when he was told by a philosopher in the crowd that one of his henchmen was plotting against him. Speechless with surprise, he had the informer executed. Dio also tells us how Caligula, toward the end of his reign, became outright hostile to the crowd assembled before him. He no longer granted them any favors but even went so far as to be completely opposed to whatever the people wanted. They responded by refusing to support any of his wishes. So, this time an angry ruler was faced with a hostile crowd. But the contest was an unequal one. The people could only shout out their opinions and make gestures. The emperor possessed ample military force. The emperor was once so infuriated when people jeered his favorite charioteer that he had soldiers kill and arrest spectators in the stands. Famously, he wished that the crowd possessed a single neck by which he could kill it, rather like the message Commodus sent to the senate when he displayed the severed ostrich head.[14]

It is striking how many of these stories of imperial bad behavior occur in the games. Another well-known story about Caligula is that he became so obsessed with his favorite racehorse, Incitatus, that he even used to invite it to dinner, where he would feed it golden barley. On the day before the games, the emperor sent soldiers into the neighborhood to make sure that Incitatus would not be woken up early. The horse lived in a marble stall, ate out of an ivory manger, and wore a harness encrusted with precious stones. It was said that the emperor planned to make the horse a consul, although this could well have been more a comment on what the emperor thought of the abilities of the average senator.[15] We are again hostage to our largely upper-class sources. But whether it is treating the Roman people with contempt or disrespecting the senate, Roman writers again and again turned to stories of what the emperors had done at the games to illustrate the true color of their politics.

We must be careful not to start thinking that the games always involved the crowd grumbling and moaning about their political leadership. Quite the opposite was the case. The normal course of events was for the audience to cheer on the givers of the games with gusto and enthusiasm. And why not? The games symbolized the greatness and abundance of the Roman Empire. As one Christian historian observed of the early empire, this was a time of tranquil peace, when emperors reigned long and devoted their tenure to festivals and public games and other joyful pleasures.[16] And from the people's point of view, why not reward those who had spent so much on their entertainment with their vocal support? It is precisely because complaints were not the norm that they were recorded for posterity in the sources. These were tense moments when tears in the fabric of the imperial political settlement were apparent for all to see.

The games sat at the heart of politics in the Roman Empire. Here was the place where an emperor met his people, heard their requests, and felt duty bound to respond to them. It was moral patronage: the regime rewarding the great Roman people for their continued support because they deserved it. Edward Gibbon was shocked at how a considerable share of public revenues was spent on public entertainments. He noted that in Antioch the magnificence of the games of the theater and the Circus was considered as the happiness and as the glory of the city. But it was precisely because the games both reflected political strength and also provided an arena for settling disputes that it was deemed worth devoting such great resources to them.

CHAPTER IV

Feeding the Monster

COMMODUS HAD GONE to great lengths to make his games innovative and memorable. Sourcing and supplying a rhino was just one part of this. We have seen that his extravagant expenditure cannot simply be seen as a madman's obsession. So-called good emperors like Titus and Trajan probably spent just as much money on providing lavish entertainments. They merely took care to be more sensitive to the concerns of the senatorial class and so had a better write-up in history books. The games had become a vital political forum in Roman society. This made all emperors feel it was worth putting a tremendous amount of effort into making them the best that they could be. A games industry evolved to meet these needs.

Putting on elaborate games took large investments of both time and money. A look at the sheer number of days of the different types of public entertainments in Rome gives a sense of what level of resources were being devoted to them. At the time of Commodus there were about 135 days of games in Rome per year, which was to rise by AD 354 to 176 days, of which 102 were devoted to the theater, sixty-four to the chariot racing of the Circus, but only ten to the gladiatorial combats and animal hunts of the arena. Arena combats took place primarily at the end of the year, often associated with the festival of the Saturnalia. These were the highlights of the entertainment calendar.

Organizing a successful show in the arena was a logistical nightmare. Capturing large wild animals, such as rhinoceroses, was not an easy task in a world without tranquillizer darts. Animals then had to be transported, fed and maintained, and sometimes trained. Disposing of the hundreds of carcasses took significant organization too. Hunters and gladiators had to be hired and taught the skills necessary to survive and to entertain the crowd. A steady stream of condemned criminals needed to be found. Then the show itself had to be advertised and the tickets had to be distributed. Various novelty items had to be arranged to please the audience. All in all, putting on a show was a good test of a leader. If he could manage that, then managing an empire could hardly be any more difficult.

The number of animals that were required for the largest imperial games is hard to contemplate. The London zoo, one of the oldest and largest in the world, houses approximately 19,000 individual animals. Many of these are fish, birds, reptiles, and invertebrates, leaving only about two hundred mammals. These larger animals were typically the kind of beasts that the Romans liked to display and kill in the arena. Trajan's games, where eleven thousand animals were slaughtered, emphasized just how vast the scale of the operation was. The games were spread over 123 days, meaning that the equivalent of the entire mammal population of London zoo was destroyed roughly every two days. Titus's games for the Colosseum's opening had five thousand animals shown or killed in a single day. The number of keepers and handlers must have run into the hundreds. The amount of feed required for all these animals would also have to have been mountainous. A horse, for example, needs about two percent of its body weight, or about twenty pounds, in food each day (this will obviously vary significantly according to age, size, and activity but will do as a rough estimate for our purposes). If we take a horse to have been about the average size of animal that was displayed at the games (again no more than a subjective estimate), then those five thousand animals required forty-five tons of food per day to keep them fit and healthy. No doubt some animals were starved close to show day to make them fiercer and more likely to attack, but they could not have been kept malnourished for long if they were not to appear mangy and hence unsuitable for an imperial show. The quantities of ordure that came out from the other end of this process were also clearly substantial.

The variety of animals was another vital factor in successful games. It was no good parading and hunting a succession of the same animals. The great imperial games went to extraordinary lengths to provide a menagerie of exotic beasts from all over the empire. Fifty years after Commodus, the emperor Philip the Arab held spectacular games to celebrate Rome's thousandth birthday, in AD 248. There were thirty-two elephants, ten elk, ten tigers, sixty tame lions, thirty tame leopards, ten hyenas, a hippopotamus and a rhinoceros, ten giraffes, forty wild horses, and a variety of other animals. Or a generation after that, in AD 281, Probus celebrated his victories with games involving a thousand ostriches, a thousand stags, and a thousand boars, a hundred lions, two hundred leopards, three hundred bears, as well as many others.

There was probably more than a hint of exaggeration in some of these numbers. And, again, it must be stressed that these were by no means normal games. In the provinces, we can imagine that the average animal hunt consisted of more easily produced animals, such as bulls, bears, and boars, with perhaps an occasional exotic highlight, such as Magerius's leopards. We get a sense of the problems that givers of smaller scale games had from the letters of Cicero and Symmachus. The first of these, in the late republic when he was stationed overseas, was hounded by a social contact to help supply him panthers for the games that he hoped would help him win high office. That was how you went about collecting your animals—calling in favors from your important friends. Four hundred years later, Symmachus wrote about how the bear cubs he had procured for his games had turned out to be emaciated. Then there was the crocodile that seemed to have gone on hunger strike because he was unhappy about how he was being kept. Finally a group of Saxon gladiators managed to strangle each other the night before their scheduled appearance. Symmachus's games had all gone horribly wrong.[1]

Different regions of the empire specialized in providing certain kinds of animal. Britain was known for its deer and dogs, Gaul for its bears and wolves, while Egypt was the source of hippopotamuses, rhinoceroses, and crocodiles. Traps and snares were used to capture the animals. Sometimes a goat or a dog would be tied in a pit to act as bait. Or teams of hunters on horseback would drive their prey into waiting nets and pens. The Great Hunt mosaic at the villa at Piazza Armerina includes a scene showing the capture of a rhino, which is held in a harness and is being led along by ropes. Some animals were doubtless easier to capture than others, such as stags and wild boars. Others, like bulls, could be bred.

The great cats were considered to be a real luxury, which every giver of games wanted to adorn his festival. Often these cats were captured as cubs so that they could be trained to produce an even more exciting performance in the arena. In order to capture cubs, hunters armed with lances and shields would drive the mother back while others would grab the young and throw them to horsemen waiting a few yards away, who would race off. If the mother pursued too vigorously, then they would drop one cub to calm and distract her while they made good their escape with the others. The legions provided a kind of standing hunting force, with some special units, such as the bear hunters of

Legio I near Cologne, being posted to capture animals for the imperial games and being exempt from normal military service.

Once captured, animals were put in dark cages to quieten them down and transported, in special ships if from North Africa, to menageries in Rome or nearby. The trade was profitable and in North Africa lay in the hands of various associations. One of these, the Telegenii, who supplied the leopards for Magerius's games, kept their own animal housing depots and even trained hunters to hire out to hosts if they so required. The number of animals that were needed to keep the games supplied, especially from provinces in North Africa, meant that, by the time the hunts were abolished in AD 523, entire species had been eradicated from their native habitats. It was said that the hippos had been taken from Nubia, the elephants from North Africa, and the lions had disappeared from everywhere.

Big arena shows also required large numbers of gladiators. Fighters usually squared off in single combat, which reduced the number of pairs required to fill a day's schedule. But in some of the grander imperial games, there are examples of staged micro-battles, between dozens or even hundreds of pairs at the same time. Augustus claimed that five thousand pairs fought in his various games, the same number as Trajan provided during his 123-day event. But these were the exceptions. We have seen that more normal games in Rome consisted of no more than 120. One great advantage that Trajan had in hosting his huge games was that he had a ready supply of captive manpower from his conquests in Dacia, which the games were held to celebrate. These prisoners-of-war could be easily and quickly trained up as gladiators and so meet the heavy demands of these colossal shows.

A provincial official who wanted to host a set of games obviously had no recourse to such a bottomless pit of resources. His usual route would be to contact a *lanista*, a man who managed a troupe of gladiators, of the kind memorably played by Oliver Reed in the film *Gladiator*. These managers owned their own gladiators and could also access the large imperially owned gladiator schools. The would-be games giver would have to negotiate with this manager how many gladiators he could have, how good they should be, and what price he was prepared to pay for them. The host did not have to buy the gladiators outright but could simply hire them for the show. Once the contract was in place, the manager would source, train, and deliver the gladiators to the arena.

The show itself would be advertised by sign writers who painted up notices on walls in the town. These gave basic information, such as who was giving the games and why, the number of pairs of gladiators who were to fight, and any other special perks that the audience would receive, such as awnings to protect them from the sun, the ability to watch executions, or a lottery to win prizes. One papyrus describes how a day's chariot racing was to be punctuated with a whole range of additional performers between the races themselves: singing rope dancers, gazelles being hunted by hounds, comedy acts, and gymnastics were all scheduled to appear.[2] These advertisements obviously raise questions about the literacy rate among the population. Who read these signs? Regardless of the number, the information obviously spread more widely by word-of-mouth.

The evening before a gladiatorial show would see the feast given for the performers. This last meal was open to spectators to come and watch. The tickets for the show itself seem to have been distributed via the host's patronage network and were probably free. The fact that the official hosting the games was a man of high status in the community meant that ticket provisioning was concentrated on the upper echelons of society, in accordance with Augustus's rules about seating arrangements. Only a modest percentage of tickets trickled down to the poor. On the day of the event itself, the host sat in his own box, proudly wearing the insignia of his office. A program would be provided detailing the names of the gladiators who would be fighting, their track record, and the order in which they were to appear. The form of each gladiator probably allowed spectators to gamble directly with each other, adjusting odds according to each fighter's record.

Clearly the growth in the number and size of games under the empire required a comparable increase in the size of the infrastructure that was needed to support them. Traditionally, gladiatorial games had been put on by wealthy Romans at family funerals and consisted of a few fighters at most. The size of these offerings increased dramatically particularly once their popularity meant that they became part of aristocratic political competition. Julius Caesar put on games, ostensibly to commemorate his long-dead father, where 320 pairs of gladiators fought. Amphitheaters had originally been made of wood but now huge permanent stone amphitheaters were constructed. These arenas spread across the empire and were located above all in the main military and administrative centers. Soldiers were often used to help build those located in legionary bases. There are 252 known in the western empire but only twenty in the Greek east, where other public spaces continued to be used instead.

The cost of the games also increased exponentially. As early as the second century BC, the historian Polybius states that the expenditure involved in putting on a show amounted to not less than thirty talents, or about 180,000 denarii, if done on a generous scale. Two centuries later, Martial states that even an economical show for a relatively minor official would cost 25,000 denarii. Petronius suggests that it would take 100,000 to put on a show that was so magnificent that your name would live forever.[3] By the fourth century AD, the consul Symmachus reputedly spent twenty thousand pounds of gold on his games, which would equate to about 20,000,000 denarii.

Hiring gladiators was expensive, particularly if they were free men who had volunteered for service.[4] The host could not free a gladiator if he had only rented him but he could exercise his power of life or death at the end of a fight. At a cost. He then had to pay the owner for the dead gladiator and prices could be sky high. A law implied that there would be a fine of fifty times the rental price if a gladiator is killed or injured so severely that he is unable to fight again.[5] External factors also sometimes interfered to drive up the price of gladiators. The plague under Marcus Aurelius, which continued under Commodus, led to him conscripting gladiators into the army, and prices of gladiators for games soared as a result. His response was to try to set legal limits to prices for gladiators according to their skill and experience and also to fix the maximum amount that any host could spend on his fighters.[6] His limit of 12,000 denarii seems very modest, and indeed optimistic, in comparison with the earlier figures.

Gladiatorial games had originally taken place in the Forum, where temporary wooden stands were erected. As the size of the structures that were built grew so did the risks to the crowd. In AD 27 a man called Atilius put up a large wooden amphitheater in the town of Fidenae, about five miles north of Rome. With an eye on profit more than health and safety, he had failed both to lay the foundations in solid ground and to secure the fastenings of the wooden structure above. The show was a sell-out, with interest flamed by the fact that the emperor Tiberius had for a period banned gladiatorial shows. Over 50,000 crowded into the flimsy structure. Unable to cope with the weight of so many, it collapsed leaving as many as 20,000 dead. The rich opened up their houses for the treatment of the wounded. The surviving relatives are described as arguing over the mutilated, unrecognizable corpses. As a result, the senate decreed that in the future only those eligible for the equestrian class should be allowed to put on games, since they believed that their high status would make them less greedy. They also decreed that in the future, all amphitheaters should have solid foundations. Atilius himself was exiled, which seems a lenient punishment by the standards of the day and in relation to the carnage he caused.[7]

The Colosseum was the ultimate in arena design. Seating fifty thousand spectators, it was completed by Titus's brother, Domitian, who added an extra tier and installed the complex structure of subterranean ramps, trapdoors, and

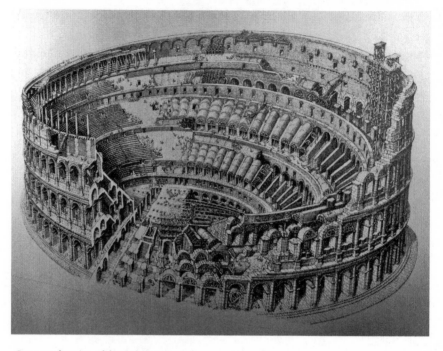

Cutaway drawing of the Colosseum

pulleys that allowed so many special effects to be enacted. He also set up the four gladiator training schools, one of which specialized in the training of animal hunters. Each had its own elliptical practice arena. The largest of these, the Ludus Magnus, was linked directly to the Colosseum by means of an underground tunnel. The Colosseum contained subterranean storage rooms for holding stage props, animals, and prisoners. Stairs from the substructure led directly to the imperial box to allow the host speedy access after the procession.

The building was faced with shining marble, while the top two levels were decorated with statues of mythological heroes and those symbols of imperial power, eagles. Each of the eighty entrance archways was numbered, and stairways led through them to the interior. The spectator had a small ticket, probably made of fired clay, which gave the number of the exterior archway entrance, the horizontal section, the wedge-shaped subdivision, and finally the row and the seat. Popularity meant that seating space was limited. Other amphitheaters suggest that each spectator was given a seat roughly sixteen inches wide and with about three feet of leg room. This compares quite closely with a modern low-cost airline, which has about the same dimensions for its seats, although allows the legs to be stretched out under the seat in front. Netting fixed on top of the wall at the front of the arena protected the crowd from escaping wild animals. In theory there was nothing to stop a net fighter from throwing his trident into the crowd, but it would have been a kamikaze move, both because it would have lost him his weapon and because it would have alienated the very people who might save him if he needed to ask for clemency.

The Circus Maximus was equally impressive. After a fire in AD 103 Trajan restored and extended the building so that it had three stories. The front rows of seats were reserved for senators and knights but the rest of the seating was unsegregated. Perhaps as many as 250,000 people could have crammed into the structure, five times as many as the Colosseum, and this represented a quarter of the population of the city. The number of races increased in line with the number of days racing until twenty-four per day became the norm. Each race consisted of seven laps, about three miles. The horses were supplied from various studs across the empire, with Spain, Thessaly, and North Africa being especially well-known for their thoroughbreds.

A long barrier ran along the center of the racetrack, the *spina*, and included a mix of monuments and shrines. At each end stood the turning posts, three bronze-covered cones, which often saw the key action in a race as the chariots bunched together to gain the maximum advantage in making a tight turn. Seven statues of dolphins and eggs stood as lap counters at each end of the *spina*. Dio tells us that Augustus's right-hand man Agrippa put them there because people kept forgetting how many circuits had been made.[8]

An Egyptian obelisk stood on the central spine, to which another was added by the emperor Constantius II in the mid-fourth century AD. This huge stone was over a hundred feet high and weighed more than 450 tons. It is the largest Egyptian obelisk to survive and now stands in front of St. John Lateran in Rome. Moving this great block of stone from Karnak across the sea and standing it in the Circus was no mean feat. The historian Ammianus describes the logistical effort it required. It was brought down the Nile by barge, where a specially constructed ship awaited it at Alexandria for the journey to Rome. This ship was larger than any ever built and needed three hundred rowers to move it. Caligula had previously built another huge ship to move another obelisk. It took more than 800 tons of lentils to serve as ballast. It was so large that his successor, Claudius, had it sunk in the port of Ostia to serve as foundations for an extension to the harbor mole. Constantius's ship sailed up the Tiber to within three miles of Rome itself. From there, the obelisk was put on a sledge and was pulled inch by inch to the Circus. It then had to be set

The huge obelisk that used to adorn the Circus Maximus

upright. So many wooden shafts were placed around it that it looked like it was surrounded by a forest of beams. So many thick ropes tied the obelisk to these beams that it hid the sky. Bit by bit, the obelisk was hauled up into the air where it hung suspended until thousands of men managed to pull it into the correct place in the center of the Circus.[9] When Pope Sixtus V relocated the obelisk to its current location in 1587, it had to be broken into three pieces to make the move possible.

It took a well-oiled recruitment system to fill these great edifices with performers. Gladiators were originally slaves, criminals, prisoners-of-war, or volunteers. Slaves could be bought specifically to be trained as gladiators, although in the second century AD some controls were introduced to limit this.[10] Criminals could be sentenced by the courts to be thrown to the beasts or given the lesser penalty of being sent to train in the gladiatorial schools. At least being a gladiator gave some hope of survival, however modest that might have been. Victory in war provided plentiful supplies of captives to fill the empire's arenas. The Jewish historian Josephus describes the fate of the citizens of Jerusalem after the city's fall to Titus in AD 70.[11] All those who were over seventeen years of age were chained and sent to the mines in Egypt. Titus also sent many as a gift to the various provinces of the empire, so that they could be executed by the sword or torn to shreds by the beasts. Those aged seventeen or less were sold into slavery. At Caesarea, Titus held special games in honor of his brother, Domitian, in which over 2,500 Jewish captives were killed fighting as gladiators or against wild beasts or were simply burnt. When Titus held games in Beirut to celebrate his father's birthday, the death toll was even higher.

In times of peace, the games needed a steady supply of criminals to satisfy the demand. The crimes that could result in being condemned to the arena included murder, treason, robbery, arson or, if a slave was involved, simply running away. Officials who wanted to put on games had to work hard to ensure that they had enough human fodder. The best criminals were those who had powerful physiques and knew how to fight. A lively semilegal trade seems to have grown up around these prisoners with hosts buying up suitable criminals for their shows. The central authorities tried to put a stop to this by insisting that the best specimens should be sent to Rome, rather than being traded in the provinces.[12] Those condemned to train as gladiators would be freed after five years' service, so long of course that they had survived. They were eligible to be awarded the wooden sword of retirement after three years. Emperors like Caligula went to bizarre extremes to meet the logistical demands of the games. He had criminals fed to the animals in his menageries to save money on butcher's meat and, when there was once a shortage of condemned criminals, he ordered his soldiers to seize a section of the crowd and throw them to the beasts waiting on the sand.[13] And in case any of them might think of crying out in protest or hurling abuse at him, he first had their tongues cut out.

Gladiators were more valuable commodities. Julius Caesar once ordered that any well-known fighter should be spared if he lost a bout and had to beg for mercy so that he could then be used in his own games.[14] After the great slave revolt of 73–71 BC had been led by the escaped gladiator Spartacus, the Roman state intervened to assume greater control of gladiator schools. This ensured a steady supply of fighters without posing the threats to security that privately run establishments could generate.

Some free men also volunteered to be gladiators. In some cases these seem to have been socially marginal individuals, such as former slaves, discharged soldiers, or retired gladiators who had been unable to reintegrate themselves into society. These volunteers were given a signing-on fee and then had to swear the gladiators' oath: that they would obey the *lanista* absolutely and would be burned, flogged, beaten, or killed if he so commanded.[15] But it was not only outcasts who signed up. Some nobles undertook to be gladiators, and even some noblewomen did. Some Italian towns seem to have tried to lure more impressionable youths from the best families into appearing in the games in order to add glamor to their provincial shows.[16] When a member of the fabled Gracchi family appeared as a netfighter, the scandal was all the greater because, as a *retiarius*, he did not wear a helmet and so his face could be seen by all. Nero seems to have channeled his hostility toward the senate by forcing many of them and their women to appear in the arena.[17] Most volunteers were probably far less high profile and so we know less about them. But we do know about one, Publius Ostorius at Pompeii, a freedman and voluntary fighter who took part in fifty-one contests.

Charioteers, like gladiators, came from similarly lowly backgrounds. Most were slaves or freedmen. As with all occupations that the Romans saw as being devoted to serving the pleasure of others, charioteers and gladiators had their legal status lowered. They suffered this *infamia* along with actors, prostitutes, and pimps. All these people had little more status than slaves. They could be treated pretty much as the *lanista* wanted, even though he too suffered *infamia*. One of the reasons that Spartacus and his troupe of fellow gladiators revolted was because they had been kept in inhumane conditions. Those who had volunteered to fight did not suffer such legal indignity so long as they remained amateurs and did not accept any cash payments.

Given these obvious downsides, we may well wonder why anyone, let alone wealthy nobles, would volunteer. The motivation of those who were down on their luck and needed the money is easy enough to understand. But those who did not need the cash seem to have been driven by a combination of thrill-seeking, machismo, and fame. One law talks about these arena wannabes as wanting to prove their manliness by fighting beasts.[18] Perhaps once the empire had been won and there were fewer opportunities to win glory in the army, some young noblemen turned to the arena to find it in a new, urban form. It is certainly true that fighters were popular. The crowds at the games supported them fanatically. Arena culture also permeated the wider Roman world. We find gladiators and beast hunters in an extraordinary variety of places, things, and myths. Mosaics of them are widespread. They were a common topic of daily gossip, street talk, and graffiti. A clay baby's bottle at Pompeii is stamped with a figure of a gladiator, presumably so that the infant could drink in his strength and courage along with its milk. Ironically, the average life expectancy of both newborn baby and novice gladiator was probably similar: they could expect to live until their mid-twenties. Gladiators are also found on bowls, on wind chimes to ward off the evil eye, and on lamps. Stories said that their blood was a cure for impotence and epilepsy. Or that a bride whose hair was parted by a spear dipped in gladiator's blood would produce lots of children. But fame cost. The fighters paid for it in sweat and blood. And for the majority who were conscripts, not volunteers, no matter how often they won they remained social outcasts so long as they continued as gladiators. It was a contradiction that Christian writers found perverse: that the Romans loved men they considered disgraceful.[19]

Gladiators may have been a cultural elite but they were reasonably common. One calculation suggests that there were about twenty thousand gladiators in the empire as a whole and perhaps four thousand in Rome itself. This was the equivalent of three legions, a significant fighting force. It also represented over two percent of the entire young male cohort. Not all of these made it to the top. The text of the price-fixing attempt by Marcus Aurelius suggests that half of them were of second rate quality. And the vast majority of them were very much D list celebrities. Only the skillful, brave, and lucky few who managed to win a number of fights became stars. Stardom helped turn some gladiators into sex symbols, although it is worth noting that two famous graffiti from Pompeii— one stating "Celadus, heartthrob of the girls" and the other "Cresces, the net-man, puts right the nighttime girls, the morning girls, and all the others"—were in fact found inside the old gladiatorial barracks. These were not the fantasies of the girls but of two-bit gladiators themselves.

Men were not the only ones who fought in the arena. A few women are recorded as having graced, or as many traditionalist Romans thought, disgraced the games. During Titus's games to inaugurate the Colosseum, he had women hunters help in the killing of the thousands of animals that were slaughtered. One of these women is described as being dressed like the goddess Venus. Another killed a lion in a gender-bending imitation of Hercules's dispatching of the Nemean lion. His successor and brother, Domitian, also used women fighters, this time as a gimmick to fight dwarfs.[20] Such female fighters were a mark of a truly exotic spectacle. The ultimate was to have, not just any women, but high-class women appear. The satirist Juvenal, writing in the early second century AD, fiercely condemned such appearances. "What sense of shame," he fulminated, "can be found in a woman wearing a helmet who shuns femininity and loves brute force?" He was outraged that a noble woman could prefer arm pads and shinguards to jewelry and sewing. He was disgusted at the grunting a female gladiator made while practicing her thrusts.[21]

A lot of this is of course over-the-top moral ranting. To reactionaries like Juvenal, wealthy women appearing in the arena was a symbol of the moral decay of society. That is one of the reasons why we find many of the stories about noblewomen fighting as gladiators in accounts of the "bad" emperors. When Tacitus tells us that in Nero's games many distinguished ladies entered the arena or Dio that Nero had many noblewomen perform in the theater, the Circus, and the Colosseum, where they played the flute and danced erotically, drove horses, killed beasts, and fought as gladiators, then we know we are in the presence of wickedness.[22] The female fighter became an easily understood symbol of imperial excess and decadence.

A number of laws were passed that tried to prevent high-class men and women from appearing in the games. Senators were banned from fighting in the arena in 46 BC, after one of them had wanted to compete in one of Julius Caesar's shows. Eight years later, another law prohibited senators and their sons from the arena and the stage. Soon even senatorial grandsons were banned from the stage. Some laws targeted women. A decree from AD 11 stated that no freeborn woman under the age of twenty and no freeborn male under twenty-five could hire themselves out for either the arena or the stage. Two centuries later, Septimius Severus also banned women from the arena after they had appeared in a highly competitive gymnastic contest, which drew widespread ridicule. Partly these laws may be seen as symbolic attempts to reassert the traditional moral order, whereby women were expected to be demure and private. But they also probably reflected the fact that the same desire for popularity, excitement, and novelty that drove many upper-class men to appear in the arena also drove some wealthy women to do the same.[23]

Once they had signed up, all gladiatorial recruits from whatever source would enter a *ludus*, a gladiator training center. Lodging in these four imperial schools in Rome was divided into separate quarters according to the type of fighter the newcomer was training to become. The foremost gladiator in each category was named the *primus palus*, the first sword. Commodus had considered himself to be the leader of the *secutores*, which entitled him to a special room in the Ludus Magnus. The new recruit was then assigned to a trainer who would educate him in his specialist skill. The imperial schools were huge centers, containing hundreds of gladiators of all levels. They provided institutional support in all kinds of ways, from masseurs to armorers, morticians, and accountants. The great Roman doctor Galen began his career as a medic in a provincial gladiatorial school. The school became the gladiator's *familia*—his home and a place where the camaraderie was probably high.

It is not clear what rules applied to a gladiatorial fight. Like modern boxing, the ancient combats seem to have had strict rules about what was acceptable and what was not. It is striking that there are a number of parallels drawn in Roman sources between the cut and thrust of the law courts and the parries and ripostes of the arena. The lawyer Quintilian, for example, notes how the strokes of gladiators provide a parallel for a legal argument. If the first stroke was intended to provoke the opponent to strike back, then the second will lead to the third. If the attack is repeated it will lead to the fourth stroke, so that there will be two parries and two attacks. And the process may be prolonged still further. This fencing nature to the combats means we should not think of the fighters as weighing in heavily against their opponents. A gladiator's blows were meant to be controlled and elegant, partly in order to maximize accuracy and to save energy.[24]

Training was done with wicker shields and wooden swords both of which were twice their normal weight to encourage muscle development and control. The swords were not long but were rather short thrusting weapons designed to give greater accuracy and control when fighting close in. One writer describes the practice a trainee would do: how he would pretend he was attacking his opponent's face, then his sides, how would sometimes try and slash the knees and legs. Or he would draw back, then spring forward and attack his imaginary opponent. He would try out every kind of attack in the book. But all the time he was trying to wound his opponent, he was careful not to leave himself open to any counterattack.[25]

It was a tough training regime. Galen describes how ancient athletes would push themselves to the limit and then force feed themselves well into the night. The rigorous training promoted physical strength to the extent that some became musclebound.[26] The diet also helped put on weight. Gladiators were sometimes called *hordearii*, barley men, and their food *sagina*, stuffing, because they ate so much weight-building carbohydrates. Analysis of the bones of more than sixty skeletons from the gladiator cemetery in Ephesus, in modern Turkey, shows that this carbo-loading was the norm for fighters. They appear to have eaten very little animal protein. Instead by consuming great quantities of simple carbohydrates, such as barley and beans, they put on weight. The aim was simple; to cover their well-honed muscles with a protective layer of subcutaneous fat. Surface wounds in fatty flesh produce a lot of blood but do little damage to the more important nerves and veins below. Nor do they hurt as much. This meant that the gladiator was able to fight on if he suffered a minor wound. It may also have meant that the spectators saw lots of gore, enough possibly to have satisfied their bloodlust. So if the fight came to a decision, the crowd might have been more prepared to grant mercy to a defeated gladiator who had clearly suffered a dramatic but actually fairly superficial wound.

The problem with a carbohydrate-rich diet of barley and vegetables was that it left the gladiators deficient in calcium. This was a problem because calcium helps keep bones strong, vital for gladiators because their heavy muscular development and weight gain needed a sturdy skeletal structure to support it. To combat this, they took supplements in the form of bone and wood ash, which is rich in calcium. However unappealing this may appear, it worked and raised the calcium levels in the bones from Ephesus to well above those of the general population.

But muscle and fat alone were not enough to make a successful gladiator. Nor was skill with the sword. Psychological strength was needed to cope with the stress of the combat environment. One Christian orator likens the Christian's struggle against the devil to a gladiatorial combat, one that will take complete focus to win. "Look at the combatants in the games," he urges his flock, "Do they worry about how they walk or what they look like? No, they ignore all such things . . . all they care about is one thing: to injure their opponent and not to be wounded themselves." As another Christian writer explains, in gladiatorial combats the winner triumphs not because he is strong but because his opponent is weak.[27] Maintaining such concentration in such a difficult environment must have taken great mental strength. Gladiators are characterized by other ancient writers as being desperate, hopeless men, fearing that they are destined to die by the sword. That may not have applied to the minority of more motivated volunteers, but we can easily imagine that many of the run-of-the-mill fighters were psychologically weakened by the constant fear of what awaited them. Their minds were "tossed between hope and despair" according to Augustine. Another describes how miserable were gladiators, how they would hang out in taverns getting drunk awaiting their expected fate.[28]

Other performers in the games also required a great deal of training. Some of the acts in the theater involved tightrope walking or physical movements that were beyond belief.[29] Some of the animal performers also took considerable training. This might be carried out to improve the cruel ferocity of the manner in which they tore their victims apart.[30] This training was carried out by groups such as the Telegenii who had organized the four leopards for Magerius's show. These professional animal traders were intimately involved in providing the material for a successful wild beast hunt, especially in North Africa where this form of entertainment was much more popular than gladiatorial contests. Organized under the patronage of a deity, in the case of the Telegenii this was Bacchus, they even had a group lucky number—three—that is seen on some of their mosaics. It was presumably unlucky for the leopards that there were four of them.

The kind of training carried out by groups such as the Telegenii met all the needs of the aspiring host. They supplied beast fighters who would, as is pictured in Magerius's mosaic, turn up dressed in brightly colored clothes. Or rather they were half-dressed so that their rippling muscles could be appreciated by the crowd. One of them, called Spittara, is even fighting a leopard while standing on a pair of stilts. This was a kind of killer acrobatics designed to thrill the crowd. He is shown successfully spearing in the throat a leopard ironically called "Victor."

The staging suggests that the Telegenii not only supplied the leopards but had also trained them, adding to the excitement. Leopards in the wild are solitary beasts who will instinctively keep away from humans rather than attack them. They are more likely to have cowered in the shade of the arena perimeter wall than attack these snazzily dressed performers. Perhaps they had been captured as cubs in the manner described earlier or had even been bred in captivity. Either way, by training them to attack men the Telegenii could ensure that the show they provided would be far more dramatic and exciting to the crowd. No one wanted to see these prize animals simply speared in the corner where not everyone could see it taking place.

The chariot racing of the Circus also demanded a steady supply of trained horses. Bred, as we have seen, on stud farms throughout the empire, the cognoscenti of the racing knew their pedigrees and took great interest in their conformation. The usual race involved four-horse chariots where the horses needed different characteristics to perform best. The inside horse needed to be the strongest to take the pressure exerted when spinning round the tight turning posts. The outer horses had to be the quickest to make up the extra ground. The two tied to the chariot in the center could be steadier, more plodding types.

The horses were supplied by one of the four racing groups known as *factiones* (factions) who provided the institutional support for chariot racing. The factions were known by the colors their charioteers wore: the Blues, the Greens, the Reds, and the Whites. With twenty-four races of eight chariots (two per faction) per day the norm, the factions needed to provide over 750 horses for a day's racing, assuming that each horse only ran the once. The sixty-six days racing per year by fourth-century AD Rome meant that several thousand are likely to have been required to take into account rest, injuries, and retirements. These animals needed to be trained, stabled, and fed. The factions also trained the charioteers. The factions became more important given the growth in the games and their political prominence. As a result, the factions became imperially controlled and owned.

Driving a chariot took great skill and practice. The racing chariot was light and traveling at speed could easily become unbalanced. Modern harness racing or trotting uses lightweight chariots and averages speeds of about twenty-five miles per hour. While slower than flat racing, this still represented a difficult proposition for the driver to control and position his chariot. Crashes, known as shipwrecks, seem to have been common and were a frequent theme in racing narratives and mosaics. This may reflect the fact that these tended to occur in the frantic jostling for position at the turning posts, which was one of the most exciting parts of the race and so more likely to be discussed or commemorated. The charioteer had the reins of the horses tied round his waist and steered using his own body weight. The implications of a "shipwreck" are obvious. Yanked down by the reins, he risked being squashed by his own chariot, trampled by his or other horses, or being dragged along by his loose outer horses. Mosaics show charioteers wearing protective leather wrappings on their torso and legs and a small leather helmet. They also carried a small knife to cut the reins in an emergency.

The four colors of the factions made the races easy to follow. It also made betting straightforward, although there is no evidence of any organized bookmakers. Most gambling probably took the form of simply striking an acceptable wager with your neighbor. The colors were coupled in the popular imagination— the blues with the reds and the greens with the whites—which may have made such one-to-one betting easier. Aficionados could obviously adjust their odds according to their informed assessment of the horses and the drivers. Everyone else could simply bet at evens with their neighbor and come out close to all square over the long run.

Tactics were all important in the race itself. Horses could be held up to come with a late run or the charioteers could try to stay in front by holding the inside track. We have race statistics from a number of surviving monuments to dead charioteers that detail their lifetime records. The most famous of these relates to a charioteer from Lusitania, modern Portugal, called Diocles. He competed for twenty-four years during the reigns of Hadrian and Antoninus Pius in the second century AD, before retiring at the age of forty-two. An inscription dedicated in his name lists him as having 1,462 wins from 4,257 runs.[31] Of these wins 815 had come from his taking the lead and holding on, 502 in a final dash, and 67 by coming from behind. He had his favorite horses because he had nine that he won a hundred races with and one with which he won over two hundred.

Sometimes the horses needed patching up after the race. An ancient text by Pelagonius, *On Veterinary Art,* details the kinds of injuries horses could sustain: it includes blows to the eyes from an opponent's whip, cuts to the tongue from pulling too hard on the bit, and injuries from being hit by chariot wheels. The horses' tails were usually tied up to prevent them getting tangled in the reins.

Gladiators also often needed patching up after fights. The quality of the medical help available was variable. During Galen's four years as doctor at a gladiator school, he claims only two died from their injuries compared with sixty during his predecessor's term. Galen also talks about the problems of replacing intestines hanging out through gaping wounds. Some of the injuries could be crippling, with a particular kind of four-pointed dagger being used to rip out the ligaments of the knee.

Head wounds are a frequent occurrence among the skeletons unearthed in Ephesus. Eleven of the sixty-eight individuals exhibit a total of sixteen well-healed cranial injuries that had been suffered in previous combats. Five of the skeletons had multiple wounds. Ten had cranial wounds that occurred at the time of death. This was despite the fact that all gladiators apart from the netman wore helmets. Three of the skulls had been punctured by tridents. The surviving gladiatorial equipment from Pompeii is highly ornate and shows no signs of any damage. This suggests that these showy helmets were used solely for the procession and not for the fight itself when plainer protection was worn. One possible explanation could be the ritual deathblow that was inflicted on a dead gladiator by an official dressed as a god in order to check that he was not faking it. It is also interesting that the bodies do not seem to have suffered multiple wounds of the type commonly observed on victims of medieval battles. This reflects a more orderly, rules-based fighting that effectively controlled and limited the violence.

A gladiator only made it to the treatment room if he had won or been spared. If his plea for clemency was turned down, then he had to be trained how to die properly. We saw in the first chapter how a defeated fighter was meant to die, head back, staring fearlessly ahead, awaiting the victor's sword. Cut marks have been found on the vertebrae of some of the skeletons at Ephesus, which resulted from the downward stabbing motion of a sword being driven through the throat into the heart. These final rituals were learned alongside how to deliver the final blow itself. The school covered all eventualities. There appears to have been some variations in how the coup de grace was given. Some scenes in art show the loser kneeling quietly with his hands behind his back. In other cases the sword was plunged in the loser's back. Perhaps different schools had their own trademark way of dying?

Another probable gladiator graveyard has been found in the Roman city of Eboracum, modern York. Part of a larger cemetery, the excavations unearthed eighty burials, of which sixty were almost complete. All were male, were on average an inch taller than the typical male in Roman Britain and were heavily built. It is possible that the group were executed criminals or soldiers who had died in battle or even a religious group with strange burial practices. But other evidence points to their being gladiators. In a third of the specimens, one arm was at least a quarter of an inch longer than the other, suggesting one-sided work such as sword-practice from an early age. As a major military and administrative center, York had an amphitheater where gladiatorial combats were held. The skeletons exhibit the same blunt force wounds as do those in Ephesus. Large carnivore toothmarks, perhaps from a bear or lion, have been found on the pelvis of one victim. This suggests either an animal hunter or someone who has been executed by being thrown to the beasts. Most interesting, forty-five of the skeletons appear to have been decapitated. This may be evidence of execution or could reflect another local form of delivering the coup de grace.

Dead gladiators had to be replaced. But is very hard to know what kind of life expectancy the average gladiator had because there are minimal data. Of the hundred or so bouts involving two hundred fighters known from inscriptions and tombstones in the first century AD, there are nineteen recorded deaths. A one in ten chance of dying is perhaps lower than we would expect in what is often assumed to be a fight to the death. Those odds seem to have worsened in the next two centuries to one in four. This may have been because the crowd became more bloodthirsty or may simply be the misleading result of the small sample size. Either way, it is clear that in a substantial majority of contests, both of the gladiators survived. The median age of death on tombstones of gladiators found in Italy is twenty-two and a half years, which compares with a probable life expectancy of a normal seventeen-year-old of forty-nine years. But tombstones by definition have a bias toward the unsuccessful and the sample size is again small.

Like modern boxers, gladiators did not fight that often, partly because there were not that many gladiatorial shows in the year, with perhaps two or three fights a year being the norm. This would have meant that on average a gladiator lived for four to five years after he began fighting. Three-quarters of the dead fighters mentioned in Pompeii have had fewer than ten contests. Many would have been saved by injuries. The fact that fighters were often from the same school, their *familia*, might have meant that fighters were not always out to get the kill at all costs, merely the win, which could be obtained by wounding. Or perhaps all feelings of camaraderie went out of the window once the fight was on. The more the gladiator fought and the more famous he became, the more likely he would be spared if he lost. The crowd would call for mercy for their favorites, and gladiators were, in any case, expensive for the host to replace. Many such gladiators were spared on multiple occasions. One called Flamma, according to his tombstone, lived for thirty years, fought thirty-four times, won twenty-one times, fought to a draw nine times, and was defeated (and spared) four times. Defeat did not always mean death. But, according to one calculation, it did for about eight thousand young men each year.

Risk brought rewards. At least it did for the lucky few. Charioteers could earn extraordinary quantities of money. The prize money for chariot races was high, ranging from fifteen to sixty thousand sesterces. Juvenal complains that a chariot driver could earn a hundred times the fee of a lawyer.[32] The famous Diocles won a total of 35,863,120 sesterces in prize money by the age of forty-two. The popularity and regularity of the circus games probably meant that charioteers were the big money sports stars. It is not surprising that we find some charioteers attempting to use magic against their opponents to try to improve their chance of success.[33]

Few gladiators made it to retirement. Even when they did, some were so addicted to the thrill of the fight and the fame, or perhaps so institutionalized by life in the schools, that they volunteered to fight again. We can imagine that the quiet life was hard to adjust to. Racehorses, by contrast, are described as loving the peace and quiet of retirement after they had left the Circus, and neither "constant fear nor doubtful palms of victory distress them." Instead they were haltered to peaceful stalls, oblivious of the restless rivalry that had once prevailed around them.[34]

New fans were the real lifeblood of the games. The arena certainly never had any trouble attracting new followers. Augustine famously describes how a friend of his, called Alypius, who utterly detested the gladiatorial shows was reluctantly taken to some by a group of friends. He was so adamant that he wanted nothing to do with them that he shut his eyes. But he could not close his ears. As one of the fighters fell, a mighty roar went up from the crowd. His curiosity got the better of him and he opened his eyes to see what had happened. He was hooked. As soon as he saw the blood, he could not turn away but stared in utter fascination. He had become one of the fanatical crowd, watching and shouting with excitement. Naturally Augustine has a Christian agenda to push here, and his story is no doubt something of an exaggeration of the sudden draw that the games could have on the individual. But it is clear that most Romans loved the games and, as they went home after the shows in the theater, the Circus, or the amphitheater had finished, they looked back at the day's events, "rejoicing in them as if they were sweet."[35]

CHAPTER V

Win the Crowd

COMMODUS SPENT A FORTUNE on his games. He was desperate to please the crowd. We have seen that one of the reasons for this was the centrality of these shows in the political process in imperial Rome. But what was this crowd? Was it just an incoherent rabble as some of the Roman elite would have us believe? Was it comprised of the lowest levels of society, the kind of people who bayed for blood and cruelty and had not a civilized bone in their bodies? A century ago, the great German historian, Ludwig Friedländer, described the Roman crowd as "a proletariat, more corrupt and wilder and rougher than in modern capitals, composed of the dregs of every nation," and as a "mob" that consisted "mostly of idlers." It is a view that was most famously articulated by Juvenal's description of how the great Roman people, who had once granted military powers and sent out the legions, had under the empire become interested in just two things: bread and circuses. How accurate was this characterization?

The first point to raise is which crowd are we talking about? Do we mean the crowd in the Colosseum, the Circus, or the theater? There were substantial differences in the social composition of each of these audiences, which might have significantly altered their character and behavior. We have seen that the Colosseum in particular did not house a neat cross section of the Roman population. It was heavily weighted toward the top half of society. Augustus had legislated to restrict the audience at the gladiatorial combats to largely the more respectable elements of the Roman people. He had also dictated where each social class should be seated. In the Colosseum, perhaps as many as 80 percent of the seats were filled by the well-off, with only 20 percent being reserved for the urban poor and women. This was more like opera than football.

The arena audience became a microcosm of respectable society. After the civil war of the late republic, Augustus was keen to reestablish social order and norms. Controlling the crowd at the highlight of the entertainment calendar was a way for him to symbolically make this clear. He made sure that all sections of society were included, but in a way that also spelled out their place in the social hierarchy. The well-ordered, rigidly arranged crowd was how he wanted his empire to be seen after the political and social chaos of the previous generation. The gladiators became the special treat he gave to the cream of the Roman people as a way of rewarding them for their loyalty and good behavior. It was a reward that was doled out according to social importance, weighted to reflect each group's significance in the Roman order. Not surprisingly, the crowd was nearly all male. A later Christian writer described the formal manner in which the various priests and officials ritually took their allotted seats after the opening procession: the colleges of all the priests and magistrates took their place, then the head Pontiffs, the Quindecemviri, crowned with wreaths of laurel, and the Flamines Diales with their miters; then the Augurs and the Vestal Virgins; and finally the whole people and the senate took their places, including the former consuls, who were "most worthy of reverence." It sounds more like a cathedral service than a rowdy sports contest.[1]

The crowd at the Circus was very different. For one thing it was much bigger: five times as big as the great Colosseum. Apart from a section at the front reserved for senators and equestrians, the crowd was a mix of all the classes and both sexes. This represented about a quarter of the entire population of Rome. Slaves could attend, but it is likely that they were underrepresented as their owners would not have wanted them to waste their time lounging at the races. Given that perhaps 30 to 40 percent of the population of Rome was servile, the crowd at the Circus Maximus was comprised of 35 to 40 percent of the entire free population. The largest modern audiences for sports events held within a stadium are rarely more than a hundred thousand and represent a far smaller percentage of the population of the cities where they are held. The Circus crowd in Rome was a real mass. Almost by definition, a crowd of this magnitude represented a reasonable cross section of free Roman society as a whole. It made for a much more volatile and relaxed atmosphere, as is attested to by the poet Ovid who used the Circus as a place to carry on a love affair.

The Circus crowd seems to have been every bit as passionate as that of the arena. The long rows of banked seats were stuffed full of fans who were intently focused on the chariot racing before them. It seemed like a mania. At the climax to each race they shouted out, urging their team on and cursing if they lost. They clapped and shrieked as loudly as they could, jumped up and down, bent down, stretched out their arms as though they could reach the course, gnashed their teeth, groaned, and threatened. The winning chariot aroused a thunderous applause, which echoed over the deserted streets of Rome and struck the ear of the traveler, when Rome had long vanished from sight. One man got so excited that he wrapped up his head in a towel because he could not bear to watch. And when the horse won, he fainted and had to be sponged back to consciousness.

The crowd at the theater was different again. The theater audience was mixed like the Circus, with the best seats in the house being reserved for the top echelons of society. The sexual content of many plays meant that the atmosphere at the theater seems always to have been pretty louche. Plutarch tells the story of how the dictator Sulla once went to a theater, which was being used to host some gladiatorial contests in the days before there were any permanent amphitheaters, and found himself sitting in what seems little more than a pick-up joint.[2] He was sitting close to a woman of great beauty and high birth, who was recently divorced. As she passed along the row behind Sulla, she rested her hand upon him, plucked off a bit of fluff from his cloak, and then carried on to her seat. Sulla was fairly taken aback at this, but she simply said, "It's nothing, I just want to share a bit of your good luck." Sulla liked this reply and fancied her and so he found out who she was. They then sat there, making eyes at each other, swapping smiles, and in the end got engaged, not, Plutarch thought, out of any chaste motive but because he was thunderstruck by her good looks and lusted after her disgracefully.

The second-century AD writer Dio Chrysostom was shocked at the crowd behavior in both the Circus and the theater at Alexandria. Whenever people entered the place, he complained, they lost all consciousness of their outside life and were not ashamed to say or do anything. They constantly jumped about, screaming and fighting with each other, and swore dreadfully, even cursing the gods themselves. They ripped their clothes off and threw them at the charioteers who lost, to the extent that they would sometimes end up leaving the show naked.[3]

Crowds as a whole behave in a variety of different ways. They can be cruel one day and lenient the next, calm and orderly in one context and violent and aggressive in another. We should not expect the Roman crowd to display a single fixed reaction to any of the events of the games. Individual crowd members also do not always behave in the same way. We saw in the previous chapter how Augustine's friend, Alypius, altered his personality in a way that fitted in with the expectations of those around him. We should also bear in mind that being a member of the crowd at the games was only one source of social identity. Accountants can be football hooligans too. But what is also clear is that the games meant a huge amount to the Romans and being a member of the crowd generated powerful emotional experiences, deep feelings of connection with what was thought to really matter in life, and a sense of purpose and empowerment. No crowd was simply just some passive lump, soaking up what was put before them like ancient couch potatoes.

In fact we find that the crowds were almost constantly active. The games were a place of political dialogue between the emperor and his people, but that did not mean they simply agreed with his point of view. It takes two to dialogue. What the crowd did have to do, though, was adopt a new kind of language to express their own opinions to those in authority. By the time of Commodus, they could no longer vote in the public assemblies as they had during the days of the Roman Republic. They had to use the rituals of the games to make their views known. We have seen already how important acclamations were to the powerful. They gave the elite a sense of legitimacy about their position in society. The fact that this is what the emperors wanted meant that this is what they usually got at the games. The people nearly always gave them the standing ovations they so craved. But occasionally the people would hold back their applause in what was a powerful critical comment on their rulers. Other collective actions such as chanting and clapping in unison, shouting out complaints, hurling abuse, and whispering gossip could all also be used to express public opinion.

The crowd took advantage of this political dimension to use the games as a mouthpiece to vent their own frustrations. The people were not mere political pawns, nor were they apolitically interested in bread and circuses alone. The crowd expressed their own political views strongly on some occasions. Food crises were a situation in which we often find the crowd shouting out their complaints during the shows. On one occasion, when the corn supply to Rome was disrupted, protests broke out in the theater. The historian Tacitus records that these were "more vocal than usual," implying that this kind of public protest was how people normally responded to food shortages. The political nature of the games provided an officially sanctioned space for such complaints to be brought out reasonably safely into the open. An emperor was obliged to listen to his people. By generating a groundswell of public opinion, the collective voice of the Roman people could then pressure the emperor into responding to their concerns and doing something to alleviate their situation. It was a way of turning the emperor's own image of Super-Patron against himself, in effect saying that, if he was the great and generous ruler he claimed to be, then he should also be able to sort out these problems for his people.

The fact that people did not always follow the script, applauding and cheering on cue like some kind of studio audience, suggests that they were not always completely sincere in their normal acclamations. There was certainly nothing spontaneous about many of the organized, well-known chants that were uttered at particular points in the games. Most of the time, it did not matter whether the people were sincere or not. Like people living in North Korea or other similarly oppressive regimes, they were obliged to go along with the political rituals for reasons of personal security. But imperial Rome was not a modern totalitarian state, nor were its people politically cynical in the way that a people can be today. But the Roman crowd clearly was capable of critical thought and skepticism and that could sometimes be aimed at their leaders as well. They would demand that corrupt officials be kicked out of office, that wars be stopped, and that food crises be sorted out. But they would not complain like this often. The emperors probably welcomed the occasional complaint about a problem that mattered to the people, because it gave them an opportunity to show off their generosity and power by fixing it.

Sometimes the people could be politically manipulative. Pliny tells us that when people heard that the emperor was coming they would gather and cheer him in the hope of getting some gifts in return. They even taught their children the formula to chant. It sounds as if the people were cleverly massaging the imperial ego in order to get something for free. We should be careful not to fall for these chants in the same way the emperors did. The fact that the ruling elite had made such a mess of Roman politics in the late republic, causing the deaths of tens of thousands of ordinary Romans, should make us alert to the possibility that the people did not automatically accept their rulers' legitimacy or claims to good governance. The ritual chants were just that—rituals.

The kind of issues that bothered the people also shows that the crowd did not always behave like mindless, aggressive hooligans. The crowd's complaints reflected the primary concerns of the people: getting enough to eat, a share of the life of leisure, and just government. The crowd had a profound interest in making sure that it got its own snout in the trough of empire. The Roman people also demanded the respect that was due to them. This respect and these benefits were given to them in the form of bread and games. It is easy to dismiss these as being politically meaningless, but they represented a substantial allocation of imperial resources. Like Juvenal, we instinctively feel that it must have been better under the republic when the people could vote and appoint generals. But it was only ever a relatively small number who could actively participate in politics in this way. And, by the time of the emperors when Rome was a million strong, such traditional political forms had become meaningless to the vast majority of Roman citizens both in the city itself and to those spread across the empire as a whole.

This was not resistance to the regime. This kind of public protest was an acceptable way for the people to express political opinions and to persuade their imperial patron to intervene on their behalf. Of course, complaining was not a tactic that the people could employ too often for fear of provoking a violent backlash. Nor could they push it too far. Josephus records a demonstration at the Circus in which the crowd called for Caligula to cut taxes. Caligula was not amused. He ordered his soldiers to kill anyone who carried on protesting and, quite sensibly, the moment the people saw this happening they stopped shouting and got a grip on themselves. They could see that there was no point pressing the issue any further. If we think about the crowd's attitude toward an emperor as an index of his popularity, then it is perhaps no coincidence that Caligula was assassinated soon after. But when people did turn to violent protest, it usually seems to have been successful, with over three-quarters of the occurrences that we know about resulting in the authorities granting the crowd's wishes.[4]

The audience at the games was also a group of sophisticated and critical consumers. For one thing, they knew the rules backward. If they suspected there had been any breech in the normal rules of the Circus, they would wave their togas and demand that the race be restarted. Some obviously began to abuse this privilege, as races were being rerun as many as ten times, so Claudius limited the number of restarts that was permitted. Or, if during the opening rituals a dancer stopped suddenly or the music fell silent at the wrong moment, then the crowd complained that something had been done contrary to sacred tradition and asked for it to be redone.[5]

The historian Ammianus complains that the people in Rome devoted their whole life to the games (as well as drink, gambling, brothels and pleasure in general). He says that their "temple," the place that was the center of all their hopes and desires, was the Circus Maximus. On race days, they would rush to the Circus at first light, having spent a sleepless night anticipating the results, and would argue vociferously among themselves about what were the best tactics for each driver to pursue.[6] During the races they would shout out tips to the drivers and, given that it is highly unlikely that the charioteers would have been able to hear them above the roar and clatter, they would reinforce their suggestions by gesticulating wildly. They knew the names, families, and cities of charioteers. Fans knew what strengths each possessed and could even give a detailed description of the good and bad qualities of all the horses. The crowd knew the horses' ages, their pedigrees, and their breeding, even going so far as to know their very grand-sires and great-grand-sires. And they knew it from memory and could recall it with great speed.[7]

By becoming so fanatical, the crowd generated its own communities of experts. Their endless talk about the races and fights turned the shows into a cultural resource, with which they could help create their own identities. It bound them together as a group. The crowd could also apply such critical faculties to their political leaders. Once, they complained that Nero was taking too long over lunch and so was preventing the games from starting. He threw out his napkin from the imperial box to signify that he had finished and that the games could begin. The people enjoyed this so much that dropping a napkin became the normal way to start races. Lesser officials were also sometimes too slow for the crowd's liking. Tertullian describes how when the praetor took too long to choose the lots for the starting gates, then the spectators would roll their eyes in impatience. The audience was also very alert to any possible match fixing. "He's thrown it," they would shout if a charioteer seemed to have too easily lost his chance.[8]

The crowd sometimes took advantage of the more relaxed atmosphere of the games to disrespect all the core institutions of Roman life. One writer talks about how irreverent the lower classes were at the games. The Circus would resound with their sneers and curses. Commodus too came in for some mockery. Although the people regularly applauded him as if he were a god whenever he appeared before them as a gladiator, he became convinced that he was being laughed at and gave orders that these people should be killed by the marines who sat up in the top tiers so that they could unfurl the awnings. Was this just paranoia on the part of the emperor? Or could he sense the lack of sincerity and the hint of laughter in the audience's cheers-cum-jeers?[9]

The crowd could also be pretty random when it wanted. People did not only protest violently about important issues such as the food supply or politics. Some riots seem to have been little more than people getting carried away. One law refers to groups of youths, who misbehaved at the spectacles and in some cities started up disruptive chants and acclamations.[10] The fight in the amphitheater at Pompeii in AD 59 between the people of Nuceria and Pompeii, where many people died, arose from what the historian Tacitus calls "a trifling incident at a gladiatorial show." The two groups of townsfolk started taunting each either, then the abuse turned into stone throwing, and finally swords were drawn.[11]

The fight at Pompeii underlines just how the people in the crowd could be violent, competitive, and loyal to their neighborhood. Spectators were used to violence and could take great pleasure in it. One advert for a show proclaims that ten bears will be killed, cruelly. Such people were also aggressive in their dealings with each other. They are described as hanging around the public spaces in small groups, arguing violently with one another, and then splitting themselves into opposing violent gangs.[12] Slandering and vilifying your social rivals in the crowd was a normal part of Roman group behavior. The fact that the crowd occasionally, in fact rarely, managed to bury their differences and complain collectively about a particular issue merely served to underline how important those issues were. The rest of the time the crowd at the games was notorious for its competitive infighting.

The games themselves fueled this rivalry. One writer calls then, "the ever-flowing spring of squabbles." Tertullian's view was that shows always led to agitation, because where there was pleasure there was passion, and where there was passion there was competition, and where there was competition, there was arguing, anger, and bitterness. That was why, he maintained, the moment people arrived at the games they started taunting each other and hurling abuse even though they had no reason to hate the targets of that abuse. They plunged into despair if one of their favorites was unlucky, they were ecstatic if they did well.[13] The rivalry expressed itself also in attempts to do each other down with magic. These vicious spells ask of the demons that they torture and kill the opponents' horses and "kill their charioteers in a crash." Death was not enough for other curse writers: "bind, enchant, thwart, strike, overturn, conspire against, destroy, kill, break Eucherius, the charioteer, and all his horses tomorrow in the circus at Rome." Or "Bind every limb, every sinew, the shoulders, the ankles and the elbows of the charioteers of the Reds. Torment their minds, their intelligence and their senses so that they may not know what they are doing, and knock out their eyes so that they may not see where they are going."

But the crowd could also be creative. Spectators gave themselves nicknames, such as Cimessores, Semicupa, Gluturinus, Trulla, Lucanicus, Porclaca, and Salsula, which might have been meant to sound grand but actually meant something like "Cabbage-eater," "Potbelly," "Scoop," "Sausage-eater," "Piglet," and "Backbiter."[14] Presumably these made-up titles were a way for the fans to establish a special games persona for themselves, divorced from the mundane realities of their normal lives. In the games their imaginations could run riot and they could invent all kinds of fan fictions.

But most of the time the crowd seem to have been strongly normative. We see this most clearly in their attitudes and behavior toward minority or outcast groups who were brought to the arena for exemplary punishment. When the Christian Polycarp was martyred in the 150s in Smyrna, in Asia Minor, the crowd was vitriolic in its contempt for him. Once the herald had announced that he was a self-confessed Christian, the whole crowd cried out with uncontrollable fury. Here was someone who sought to overthrow their gods, who had been teaching people not to sacrifice to them and not to worship them. It would have risked offending the gods not to have punished such a man severely. The prominent role the spectators played in the drama of his martyrdom is striking. They shouted out for the governor to set a lion on him. But the governor replied that this would be illegal, because the wild beast hunts were by then finished. So they demanded that he be burned alive. When the governor approved this punishment, the crowd actually went out and gathered wood for the bonfire. And when the funeral pyre had been built, the crowd surrounded Polycarp in order to nail him to it.

These gruesome spectacles were not reserved for Christians. Nor did all Romans love them. Seneca complained that the lunchtime executions pandered to the worst kind of spectator. This was a pitiless public who wanted only to see death. They didn't care that the victim had no protective armor or weapon, since that would merely have delayed the moment of execution. It was simply a conveyor belt of death. But it is worth also noting that Seneca says that the arena was empty at this point. Obviously not completely empty, but it was lunchtime when many, perhaps most, had gone for food or a rest. So we should be careful not to taint all of the crowd with this kind of viciousness.[15]

Even if the crowd were not all as hard-hearted as Seneca suggests, the public execution of criminals served to reinforce the norms of mainstream Roman society. It reflected what most people thought should happen to these outcasts, even if not all of them delighted in watching it take place. When the poet Martial describes how one criminal was ripped apart, so that his lacerated limbs dripped with gore, and his whole body had been eviscerated, even though he knew nothing about the victim's crime let alone any mitigating factors that might have accounted for it, his view was adamant that the victim deserved it.[16] Rome, like most preindustrial societies, demanded a public retribution against those who breached its laws. The people of the crowd were content to see this take place before them. It reassured them that proper social order had been restored and that their own values had been upheld. Criminals had openly flouted those rules and so the crowd needed to see them restored to preeminence. The sovereign Roman people ritually and brutally triumphed over society's enemies.

But the crowd was also capable of compassion. In the rhetorical exercise, *The Case of the Ransomed Gladiator*, the untrained, poorly armed fighter, who had volunteered to swap with his friend in order to save him from death, says that one factor would render him as an object of pity to some: the fact that he appeared to be unevenly matched. The crowd had no interest in seeing a one-sided mismatch. They wanted a thrilling and balanced contest between equals. But as with Seneca's letter, it is also worth noting that the volunteer gladiator believes that this sense of fair play and resultant pity will only be felt by some. Many will not have spared a thought for the victims, just so long as they were entertained. In fact contests between unequals could still generate considerable interest if the underdog fought particularly valiantly, as the volunteer was himself to do. Above all, of course, we know that many losing gladiators, most gladiators in the evidence from Pompeii, were let off. As one poem states, "Even in the fierce arena the conquered gladiator has hope, although the crowd threatens with its hostile thumb."[17] Presumably the host did not always override the crowd's opinion, which in any case was likely to be unclear on many occasions, and let the defeated off the hook. The crowd must often, even usually, have wanted the losers to walk away with their lives intact.

Curiously, the Romans seem to have had a particular soft spot for elephants. During Pompey the Great's games in 55 BC, he ranged twenty of the beasts against spear-throwing hunters. But it did not go according to plan. One elephant put up a tremendous struggle and, even though its feet were badly wounded, crawled on its knees toward its attackers. It snatched away their shields with its trunk and hurled them into the air. Much to the alarm of the crowd, the other elephants tried to escape by breaking through the iron railing that surrounded the Circus where the fight was being held. But they were unable to smash their way out and, when the elephants had given up all hope of escape, they started to play on the sympathy of the crowd. They seemed to beg the onlookers with indescribable gestures, they moaned and they wailed, and so upset the crowd that the spectators stood up together in tears and hurled abuse at Pompey. There was, as Cicero said, "a feeling that the beasts had something human about them."[18]

The crowd could even show some pity for convicted criminals who were to be executed before them. When one young Christian woman who had recently given birth was stripped naked before them they shuddered to see her breasts still dripping with milk. They demanded that she be taken out of the arena and clothed in some loose garment before being brought back to face her death. Of course, this had more to do with the girl offending the crowd's self-proclaimed sense of decency. There is something bitterly ironic about the spectators being so affronted by the supposedly indecorous sight of a young mother's engorged breasts and their satisfaction in seeing her brutally tortured and ripped apart by a wild bull as punishment for being a Christian.

And not everyone loved the sight of blood. In the fictional account of a gladiatorial combat, the author describes how there are some people who "grow upset even at the punishment of condemned criminals," who "grow pale at the sight of anyone's blood, and who actually weep over the misfortunes of complete strangers." It is easy to dismiss the crowd as wantonly bloodthirsty and completely lacking in any kind of sensitivity, when this text suggests that was not the case. Admittedly, the text also describes how there are also the opposite types—those who don't even feel grief when their own relatives die.[19] But not everyone was like that.

Given the multiple aspects of crowd behavior, it is perhaps not surprising that the elite thought the crowd was volatile and fickle. The spectators often seemed to be responding differently and making surprise requests. In part this was true. The crowd was able to change its mind quickly and seemingly for minor reasons. But we should remember that the crowd's volatility was also a reflection of its own autonomy. The crowd was not simply something to be manipulated by their leaders—they thought for themselves. And in any case, perhaps if they were fickle they were simply copying the inconsistent and arbitrary decision-making processes of the emperors themselves. Nero and Caligula hardly seem to have been models of calm, rational management and leadership.

Another aspect of Roman crowds that means we should not see them as a single, consistent organism is that they were mostly divided into factions. In the Circus, spectators supported one of the four colors. Those who followed the gladiators were generally split into two groups, the *parmularii*, who backed the light-armed fighters who carried a small shield, the *parma*, and the *scutarii*, who supported the heavy-armed gladiators, who carried a long shield, the *scuta*. Partisanship in the arena appears to have been less strong or all-pervasive than it was in the Circus. This probably reflected the fact that the fighting was itself almost inherently fascinating in a way that the horseracing was not. Watching men battle it out and then face the life-or-death decision of the crowd and host was enthralling enough on its own. It may also have reflected the fact that there seems to have been considerably more betting on the chariot racing, which naturally split the crowd into backers of different runners.

Even emperors became ardent fans of the racing colors. Vitellius and Caracalla supported the Blues, but the Greens were the most imperially favored color. Caligula, Nero, Domitian, Commodus, and Elagabalus were all fervent supporters. Typical of his philosophical detachment, Marcus Aurelius was grateful that he was not a partisan of any of the four factions. Typical also was the over-the-top manner in which Caligula exhibited his support of the Greens. He would often have dinner with their charioteers and would spend the night at their stables. Nero too went so far as to have the track dyed green and wore the colors himself.[20]

The word for fan in modern Italian is *tifoso*, because the raving supporter looked like a victim of typhus. The Circus crowd in Rome seems to have been similar. They were passionate about the charioteers to an astonishing degree. Cassiodorus describes how, more than at the other games, dignity was forgotten and "men's minds are carried away in frenzy." When the Green chariot won, one section of the crowd was grief-stricken. The spectators hurled rabid insults, and even though they were not really being harmed, you would have thought they were being seriously wounded when their chariot lost. They argued vociferously with each other as if they were debating matters of national importance. Interestingly he notes that they acted as if they were engaged in some kind of mass religion, which was a clear departure from normal, decent behavior.[21]

Later, when the capital of the empire had been moved from Rome to Constantinople, this fanaticism in the Circus reached its zenith. Procopius details how the whole population was divided into two camps. They sat separately in the Circus and were so committed that they would happily have died for their color. They fought with their opponents even though they knew that it would often result in their being dragged away to prison by the soldiers, where they would be tortured and killed. They hated their rival color even though there was no reason for it. It informed all their lives and they would not marry or have friends of the other color and disowned family who supported the other faction. Nothing in heaven or on earth mattered as much to them as the games. God could be being blasphemed, the empire could be under assault, and they would take no notice because they were so engrossed with their faction. For Procopius it was "a disease of the soul."[22]

The dichotomy between the fanatical behavior in the crowd and the relative calm of normal life is a common theme in ancient sources, in the same way that sports fans today often appear divorced from their everyday existence. Partly we can see this extreme behavior as resulting from the greater license of the leisure event. People feel more able to express themselves in their free time. But it is also possible to see this as an intensified form of normal life. It is a place where the important themes and issues of everyday life are put together in a focused form that generates a powerfully concentrated reaction. We can see in the Circus, then, a reproduction in an exaggerated form of the factionality of normal life centered on the neighborhood. What were the principal characteristics of this ordinary Roman life?

Much of the social life of ordinary Romans centered on the local communities in which they lived and worked. These areas served as strong cultural and even political boundaries within the city of Rome. People looked toward their neighbors for support when times were tough. Friendly social contact in normal times would establish mutual ties that could be turned to when people needed to get help. Those who had patrons were also part of a vertically structured network that could benefit them when they were in need. Of course, help was not always forthcoming. Benefactors and neighbors would have to ask themselves whether they could spare the help, was the relationship strong enough to warrant it, would the recipients repay the favor. But such local social networks were a powerful component of most people's lives.

That does not mean that life in Rome was cosily communal. Many fables and proverbs warn about the difficulties of dealing with neighbors and the inconsistency of friends. They might steal from you or they would gossip about you behind your back. Most Romans lived crammed together in small apartments, which did not make for relaxed social relations. These tensions exhibited themselves in outpourings of local bitterness and bad blood. One lead curse tablet from near Carthage gives a flavor of the competitive, mocking, envious society the nonelite inhabited: "I, Maslik, make Emashtart melt, the place where he lives and all his belongings, because he has rejoiced at my expense about the money that I have completely lost. May everyone who rejoices at my expense about the loss of my money, become like this lead which is now being melted."[23]

Gossip and magic were a way for this envious society to police itself. It served to keep people in their place and enforce communal norms of behavior. Accusations of immoral behavior in such public inscriptions as graffiti worked to advertise offenders' weaknesses and to get them to mend their ways. A scrawl such as "Ampliatus Pedania is a thief" publicly shamed the man, making all those in the vicinity look out for his thieving hands. Consulting a magician was also a way of advertising the fact that someone's behavior was generating disquiet in the community.

This was a largely oral culture, and chat was the primary means of information exchange and opinion formation. It served to maintain status and reputation, to network, and to provide essential news about what was going on in the locality. Communal conversations also acted as a survival manual of practical advice, a resource to turn to when problems emerged. It was a society where the individual needed cunning to survive. Success in this world did not depend on good behavior. It took natural wit to keep ahead of the pack.

Above all, it took money. Maintaining income through paid employment or by learning a trade was vital for the urban nonelite to survive. Having a trade was a particularly good way to improve your life chances, because it generally paid about twice as much as working as a manual laborer. Being a baker or a carpenter or a tanner also served as a central pillar in establishing identity and status within the local community. A trade epitomized the kind of practical expertise and accrued experience that was valued among ordinary Romans and was carefully handed down from generation to generation.

We can see all of these themes epitomized in the games. The focus on the individual stars stressed their technical virtuosity and physical endurance. In doing so, the games effectively raised the attributes of the traditional Roman soldier to the status of an art form. The muscular sports star became a metaphor for Roman society: tough, disciplined, and skillful. The performers also reflected the kind of assertive masculinity that men needed to exhibit if they were to do well in life. Competitors had to take carefully calculated physical risks and perform repetitive tasks with accuracy, skill, and bravura.

We can see the focus in the arena on different types of gladiator as reflecting the trades that were so important in ordinary Roman life. Gladiators were matched so that their strengths and weaknesses balanced each other. The *parmularii* were lightly armed but mobile, whereas the *scutarii* labored under their heavy burdens. Each type relied on skills and strategies that were specific to their kind. The arena acted as a microcosm of ordinary work, with overlapping and complementary skills competing with each other to make a living and succeed. Watching various gladiators who each had specialist techniques and appearances of their own probably appealed to the many nonelite who relied on their own areas of niche expertise for a livelihood. This congruence was noted by Basil the Great who asks in one of his letters, "Are not winners in the games made famous by winning, and craftsmen by the skillful design of their work?"[24]

Statuette of a type of gladiator known as a Samnite, after
warriors from an area of Italy that the Romans conquered
in the early republic

This reliance on specialist expertise was also reflected in the way that the
fans became intensely knowledgeable about their heroes. Some spectators
knew the gladiators' records in detail. Galen describes how the partisans of the
Blues and Greens even smelled the dung of their racehorses to satisfy themselves that they were being fed good quality fodder. This kind of knowledge
helped to create a hierarchy within the crowd, identifying those who were the
real experts. These were the people who would excel both in the crowd and in
real life.

The strong competition between the fighters and the factions also reflected the vigorous competitiveness of normal life. People had to struggle hard to work their way up the status ladder. Surviving Roman graffiti is full of depictions of gladiators. It is possible to see this as a vicarious identification with the fighters who symbolized the ordinary people's own struggle to make ends meet and even improve their situation a little. This gladiator graffiti tends to contain lots of information in the form of facts and figures. Boiling down a gladiator's existence to a series of hard numbers reflected the focus on practical outcomes that the ordinary people had. What mattered were results. It also suggests that numeracy was far more important in their outlook than we might otherwise imagine. Literacy was a luxury that most could do without. The ability to count and calculate, to know how to price and evaluate were indispensable skills.

The spectators issued a constant stream of vocal commentary on how each competitor was performing. This reflected the vocal manner in which daily opinions and judgments were formed. In this Roman rat race, people had to work hard to maintain their reputations and coneal their weak points. The gladiator himself acted as a lesson in how to hide what he was really thinking. An old proverb said "the gladiator takes counsel in the sand." He had to think on his feet and keep poker faced so that his opponent had no clue what move he intended to make next. Similarly, the charioteer had to be prepared to make brave maneuvers to force rivals into colliding and coming to grief. Like the gladiators, charioteers epitomized the attributes that people needed in their daily lives: technical expertise, resilience, strength, nous, the ability to jockey for position, and to cheat. The games therefore allowed the Romans to personify popular virtues in heroic terms.

We find a symbolic equivalence between typical lower-class characters and the different types of gladiator in ancient dream interpretation. The dream interpreter, Artemidorus, explains the significance of gladiatorial dreams. His analysis is that if a poor man dreamt that he was fighting as a gladiator that was good news because it meant that he would get married. He then explains how the dream will indicate what character of woman the man will marry because it will correspond to the type of weapons that he dreams he is using or to the type of opponent against whom he is fighting. "For example," he says, "if a man fights a Thracian, he will marry a wife who is rich, crafty, and fond of being first. She will be rich because the Thracian's body is entirely covered by his armor; crafty, because his sword is not straight; and fond of being first, because this fighter employs the advancing technique." To dream of a *retiarius*, who fought with a net and trident, signified a poor and wanton wife, "a woman who roams about consorting very freely with anyone who wants her."

The division of gladiators into clear brands, based on their appearance and fighting technique, appealed to the ordinary spectators because it corresponded to the personality types they encountered in their everyday existence. The solid, active, hard worker at one end of the spectrum, personified by the *secutor*, versus the quick-witted trickster in the form of the *retiarius*. This dodgy aspect of the netman made him the most reprehensible type, even among the shameful class of gladiators as a whole. He wore no mask, which would otherwise cover his shame from appearing in public, and almost naked, and he carried inferior weapons. A trident and net were fit for a lowly fisherman not for a soldier.

The realization that the games developed in accordance with popular tastes underlines how active a part the crowd played in structuring the event itself. That does not mean, of course, that the elite had no input, that there was no place for the power of noblesse oblige or elite competition. Nor does it mean that members of the nonelite sat in on planning meetings or answered questionnaires about what they wanted to see. They didn't have to. They made it clear what they wanted by voting with their feet. And, when they were in attendance, they cheered and booed and made their feelings plain. The games revealed a lot about what the people liked, because the sponsors gave them what they wanted in return for popularity. Nobody tried to emulate Pompey's treatment of the elephants again.

Even once Italy had come under Ostrogoth rule in the sixth century AD, the Circus retained its power over the rulers of Rome. Cassiodorus, writing on behalf of King Theodoric, complains that the government is compelled to support this institution by the necessity of humoring the majority of the people, who are passionately fond of it. "It is," he complains, "always the few who are led by reason, while most people crave excitement and want to be able to forget their worries." He concludes that the elite, however much they might disapprove of the institution, must therefore share the people's stupidity on occasions and give them the free circus games that they desire.[25]

The tastes of ordinary Romans differed markedly from those of the refined upper classes. Popular entertainment was characterized by showy excess. The games were no place for modest restraint to be elegantly displayed. Tacitus complained that Rome seemed to possess its own specific vices, which were practically born in the womb. These were the obsession with actors and the passion for gladiatorial shows and horse racing. "How much room," he asks, "does a mind preoccupied with such things have for the noble arts?" Likewise, Pliny the Younger deliberately contrasts his love of high culture and learning with the circus games. These races were, for him, "an entertainment for which I have not the least taste" but were so popular that even the great metropolis of Rome was left deserted and strangely quiet while the races were on. In Pliny's eyes the circus racing had nothing to recommend it. There was no novelty or variety, nothing interesting enough that a cultured man would want to see it twice. He is even more amazed that people seem to have no interest in the skill of the charioteer, their only obsession being their loyalty to the colors of the factions. He finds this factionality utterly mystifying. He is not much less amazed that some serious-minded people are also fans of the colors.[26]

Cicero was astonished at the brutality of the animal hunts, which he saw as anathema to elite taste. "What pleasure," he asks, "can there possibly be for a man of culture to see some pathetic specimen of humanity being mangled by a powerful beast, or a splendid animal being run through with a hunting-spear?"[27] We have seen that it was only some part of the crowd that reveled in the midday executions. But the hunts were widely popular. Was it a surprise that ordinary Romans who had to survive in the competitive atmosphere of Rome liked their entertainments to be equally brutal? And in any case, the hunts were in many ways a popular reinvention and intensification of the traditional hunting that had previously been the preserve of wealthy Romans on their country estates.

Later Christian writers singled out the sexual atmosphere of the theater games in particular as being completely inappropriate for decent society. Cyprian describes what he calls the "shameless corruption of the stage." He finds the plays full of adultery, lewd behavior even by women, and rude jokes. Even the fathers were portrayed as stupid, obscene, and immodest, a shocking portrayal in a patriarchal society. He cannot understand why everyone flocked to see the plays even though everyone got ridiculed in them.[28] Augustine too was shocked to recall how in his youth he took pleasure in the obscene and filthy shows.[29] He was outraged that all this lewd behavior went on before a mixed-sex crowd. As Clement of Alexandria warned, such mingling in the theaters can only lead to desires growing warm. He called for plays that are full of buffoonery and gossip to be banned. The Christians found such sexually explicit behavior more troubling than even traditionally minded Romans did, but they too had often balked at the immodesty on display in the theater.

The people inhabited a more physical, less restrained world than the elite did, and they often took their pleasures in a bawdy and mocking way. Of course there is an element of dramatic license at work here too. The shocking nature of the plays served to underline normal rules of social conduct. But the theater shows ran for over a hundred days by fourth-century Rome so it is only possible to take that argument so far. Instead, it is simpler to see their sexual content as representing an intensified form of ordinary life, where the emphasis on sexual restraint, seriousness, and modesty was far less pronounced than among the elite.

The arena, the theater, and the Circus became the people's palaces where spectacle dominated. The way the senses were used highlighted this different attitude toward entertainment. The people liked the senses to be powerfully and dramatically assailed. Everything had to be bright, dazzling, loud, and overstated. The traditional elite found this gaudy and sensational. But, even if the games appeared to be vulgar to some high-class Romans, it was not in any way a threatening phenomenon. The people were expressing their amazement at the spectacles within an environment that was very much in the control of the emperor. The games fused the political and the sensual to form a powerful glue that could unite the different parts of Roman society.

We must be careful not to see a cultural chasm separating the elite from the masses. The games showed that it was possible for Roman society to create social forms that could incorporate everyone bar a few elitists and religious extremists. One way of achieving this cross-social conversation was for the games to draw on elements of common culture such as mythology. By reenacting well-known scenes, such as Hercules the animal slayer, emperors like Commodus were trying to manipulate the social memory. They partially reinvented such myths. On one occasion, Orpheus emerged from Hades, he enchanted nature with his playing so that animals crowded round him and even rocks and trees moved toward him; then, in a new twist to the tale, he was torn apart by a bear. The fun for the spectator lay in knowing the plot, knowing that it would be subverted but not how, and the thrill of irreverence when the twist finally came. Repeated references to such collective stories linked the emperor himself with the gods. Here was a man whose power was such that he could re-create and even rewrite mythology if it suited him. Marcus Aurelius complained that the amphitheater was boring, because it always stayed the same, but the games showed the popular preference for innovation based around well-known themes. They played with existing formats and plots to generate interest and entertainment.[30]

Convention and formula, from the procession, to the chants and the rules of the action itself, all established common ground among the spectators, whatever their social status. The crowd found this repetitive process satisfying as it did with other forms of ritual behavior, such as religion. The deeper and more detailed knowledge it ingrained in the crowd also gave people an increased capacity for understanding and enjoying the particularities of every performance. Originality was welcomed only to the degree that it intensified expected experience. Like Roman society as a whole, the audience at the games was conservative and backward-looking. It instinctively disliked any fundamental change, preferring to see in an ever-repeating set of formulas a representation of the continuities of life.

In this chapter, I have tried to reactivate the crowd and rescue it from lumpen status. The audience was not made up of mere political pawns. The emperors needed the people's support to legitimate their rule, which made their vast expenditure on providing them with spectacular entertainments a sound political investment. The performers in the shows can be seen as validating the repetitive skills, resilience, and resourcefulness of ordinary Romans. The performers also acquired a political role because of their importance as mediators in the relationship between an emperor and his people. They became powerful in their own right, deriving their strength both from imperial patronage and also from their popularity with the crowd. Many emperors, such as Commodus, liked to associate with the stars in public. Commodus and Nero went so far as to want to appear in the games because that was where real popularity lay. The games and their stars created a focal point for Roman society in which it was able to articulate its own self-image and core values. The games represented, therefore, a fundamentally decent and respectable display of societal norms. The audience was in no way the ignorant and bloodthirsty rabble it used to be accused of being.

CHAPTER VI

How to Be a Roman

IN "THE CASE OF THE RANSOMED gladiator," we have an exercise that concerned the law that a Roman father could disown his son if he had just cause to do so. The context for this imaginary tale is that two men were enemies, one rich, the other poor. But their sons were good friends. One day, the rich man's son was kidnapped by pirates who sold him to a gladiatorial school. His friend immediately set off to try and rescue him. Finding him about to enter the arena, the only way he could secure his freedom from the manager of the troupe of gladiators was to offer to stand in his place. Mismatched against a far more experienced and better-trained opponent, he stood no chance.

When the rich man's son returned home, he immediately sought out his friend's poor father. He had promised his friend that he would help the old man if he didn't make it out of the arena alive. Now he was determined to fulfill that vow. His own father was outraged. Here was his son aiding one of his enemies. He promptly cut him off. In the imaginary court case that followed, as part of his defense, the son gives a graphic account of the gladiatorial combat his friend had died in. Every detail emphasizes his friend's virtue.

His friend, an untrained novice, faced a veteran. But he did not give up hope. It was, the rich man's son said, a great shame that his courage and bravery had not been put to good use in the army. Real fighting required such energetic fervor, unlike the more constrained fencing that went on in the arena. "With what vigor did he rush out into the fray," the son describes, "enraged against his opponent as though he were still mine!" But this unfocused assault did not faze the veteran. He deftly parried every assault with a simple turn of the wrist. The poor friend would no doubt have been granted mercy if the crowd had been given a chance to express their opinion, but the veteran had been annoyed by this upstart and did not want him to live. As the novice grew tired his guard slipped and his naked torso was exposed to his opponent's blows. He received the blow that killed him, standing up, facing straight ahead. "Gentlemen," concluded his friend, "When did you ever hear of such a thing? He became a gladiator because of his virtue!"

Gladiators, remember, were legally inferior, social outcasts. The son explains that nothing had been a more crushing burden for him than to accept the title of gladiator and to submit to a trainer as his master. It was like becoming a worthless slave. Every day he had to sleep in a dingy gladiator's cell in the barracks, eat the special training diet, and practice hard. He was treated like a criminal. Yet here, in this account, we find a gladiator being presented as a paragon of virtue. Obviously, the story relies on this stark contrast to help produce its dramatic effect. But it was a paradox that was visible in arenas across the Roman Empire. Gladiators who were regarded as worthless in the eyes of society acted as symbols of Romanness at its best.

We have seen in the previous chapter that the crowd was not some passive lump. They were sophisticated consumers, whose vocal support the emperors needed to lend legitimacy to their rule. The crowd also had its own aims and sometimes used the games to help secure them. The games suited both sides in this political debate, because they drew for their effect on the broad, cross-social ideal of what it meant to be a true Roman. Drawing on themes such as honor, manly vigor, and the repetitive skills required by peasants and craftsmen, the games were a story the Romans loved to tell themselves about themselves.

The emotionally charged atmosphere of the games acted as a good medium for these messages to be advertised. We might think of games as being mere idle and trivial fun, as some kind of perverse delight, but they are best understood as having represented a way for the Romans to construct their community through the expression of core values, above all masculine and military virtue. The short and dramatic scenes of competitive sport allowed for these powerful and intrinsic themes of Roman society to be focused with an acute intensity. It made them more clearly visible and expressed them in a purer form than could ever happen in the messy complexity of normal life. The ancients themselves noted how exaggerated a form were the gladiatorial combats in comparison with daily life: "Fortune offers the gladiator one alternative: either to kill, if he wins, or to die, if he loses. But the life of men in general is not constrained by such unfair or inevitable necessities that they must be the first to commit an injury so that they can avoid suffering injury."[1] The contests in the arena and the Circus taught you what you had to do to be a success in the Roman world. It showed you how you should respond to failure and what happened to the defeated. All in all, the games can be seen as lessons in how to be Roman.

Traditionally, the games have been regarded as an expression of Rome's violent and homicidal tendencies. To see the games as a physical enactment of collective ideals does not mean we now have somehow to approve of them. But it does mean we should try and understand them on their own terms and not simply superimpose a black-and-white moral template onto them. The games were seen by nearly all Romans as a good thing. They saw them as civilized, urbane, and sophisticated. By definition, if we are going to try to understand something of the Roman way of thinking, we are going to have to shift to a more nuanced, Technicolor view rather than simply dismissing them as almost psychotically violent.

The games can perhaps most easily be understood as a contemporary remodeling of traditional Roman military ideals. When gladiatorial combats were first introduced, they involved prisoners-of-war, who fought with their own weapons and in their own particular fashion. So Samnites captured from Campania in what is now southern Italy, Galli from Gaul, and Thracians defeated in northern Greece were made to fight wearing what at the time seemed outlandish costumes, carrying peculiar weapons, and in their own particular style. There may have been some sense of mockery at work here. The victorious Romans laughing at the bizarre fighting techniques and armor of these losers, factors that they doubtless thought had contributed to their failure in the first place. The Roman audience was in those days very likely to have served in the legions themselves and so were knowledgeable and critical observers of the fighting techniques of others. Once the gladiatorial combats had become popular and combatants were being specially selected and trained, we can imagine that mockery turned into a grudging respect for these worthless men skilled in the bloody arts of hand-to-hand combat.

Respect had to be earned. The watching crowd had no sympathy for any gladiator who did not fight like a man. As Cicero said, in gladiatorial combats, where the fate of the lowest classes of mankind is concerned, "it is natural in us to dislike the trembling suppliant who begs to be allowed to live, but we are eager to save the courageous and spirited who hotly fling themselves at death."[2] Even later Christian writers understood what made a good gladiator. Born in the fourth century AD, John Chrysostom explains to his flock that they should suffer whatever great evils the Lord throws at them with silence and fortitude.

Like those that they applaud in the games, they should not worry if they suffer defeat but should hold their head up high. They must not run away after the first exchange of strokes. The crowd loves those who fight manly and nobly, but it laughs at those who are pathetic cowards. If any gladiator were to run off at the mere sight of his opponent raising his sword, he would be mocked as feeble and effeminate and inexperienced.[3]

Disciplined self-control was a central facet of this display of virtue. Gladiators were often thought of as men who were free from social constraints and were characterized as being reckless because of their lack of hope. But the best gladiators showed nothing of this weakness. They were models of iron discipline. They were careful not to lose their tempers because "they expose themselves to wounds when they are angry." They had to master every movement of their body and faces so as not to give away what they were thinking or intending to do. There was an old saying about gladiators that "they watch intently, so that something in the way their opponent glances, some movement of his hand, even some slight bending of his body, gives a warning of what they are about to do." This was no easy task. In a school of twenty thousand gladiators, there were supposedly only two who could stop themselves from blinking when in danger. But they were invincible as a result, because they neither missed any of their opponents' moves nor gave anything away themselves. Gladiators could be so tough that there was one who used to laugh when his wounds were probed by doctors. This was, in the writer Gellius's view, a "true and noble fortitude," of the kind that the Romans of old would have approved. Pliny describes how the gladiatorial shows "inspired a glory in wounds and a contempt of death even in slaves and animals." The training of animals to do unnatural acts, such as lions toying with hares or dogs that did not touch their prey, merely emphasized the power of disciplined training.[4]

Skill, intelligence, and experience were the competitor's best defense. Doing something stupid was dangerous, because "skill is their protection, anger their undoing." For gladiator and soldier alike, Cicero says, "it is keen and ready intelligence, endowed with sharpness and resourcefulness that secures men against defeat."[5] The idea of having closely matched and complementary opponents was a way of making sure that the fight was a true test of all these qualities. It ensured that the victor was worthy of the glory and adulation he would receive.

We find a comparable need for quick-witted skill in the animal hunts. One writer noted how popular these contests between man and beast were: "Nothing attracts people as much as men fighting animals. Escape from the beasts seems impossible, but through sheer intelligence the men succeed."[6] We also find this in the chariot racing, where the charioteer had to deploy the right tactics if he was going to be successful. In a first-century AD epic poem by Silius Italicus, we have a description of a chariot race, supposedly held at the general Scipio's victory games after the Roman success in the Punic wars.[7] Four chariots with teams of four horses each were racing, and the driver Cyrnus got off to a flying start, leaving the rest behind. The crowd roared with applause, thinking that with such a start their favorite had as good as won. But those who looked deeper and had more experience of the racecourse criticized the driver for expending all his energy at the start. They muttered various ominous warnings, saying that he was wearing out his team and that he should be keeping something in reserve. "Put down your whip and tighten your reins," they shouted. But Cyrnus did not listen. He sped on, without sparing the horses, forgetting how much ground had still to be covered. The result was as those naysayers in the crowd had predicted. The other drivers held up their teams and preserved their energy. Cyrnus's team started to tire. Desperately, he tried to block the other chariots' attempts to overtake him by swerving across the track. But soon he was left behind. Too late was he learning "the wisdom of controlling his pace."

The games revealed the inner characters of participants because it showed how well they performed under pressure. It made it clear whether they possessed the manly qualities of the Roman military tradition. Nowhere was this more apparent than in the arena because of the presence of death. It made the consequences of failure and of failing to live up to expected standards of behavior a vitally important matter. The moment of death, when the defeated gladiator had been declined mercy and was ritually executed by his triumphant opponent, was thought to be the peak moment of character display. It is a common scene in Roman art for that reason. We have seen how the gladiators were trained to die properly. This was the ultimate expression of self-control, to willingly and steadfastly bare your throat to another's sword. Even emperors took a morbid fascination in these dying moments, with Claudius being particularly keen to watch the death agonies of the defeated.[8]

The spectators expected those who had to die to do so without hesitation. They grew angry when those defeated in battle did not.[9] They gesticulated and jeered and felt that they had been robbed of their favorite bit of the spectacle. They thought it was quite simply wrong for a gladiator not to die cheerfully, because it was considered an honor for these worthless individuals to appear before the great Roman people. Death was also important because it gave one final chance to those who had failed in the fight to rehabilitate themselves in the eyes of the crowd. There was nothing to fight for now, no hope of safety. Why not

Defeated gladiator being put to death to the accompaniment of horns

show in the way that they died that they were actually brave men? Seneca noted that when faced with death some men discovered newfound courage: "For death, when it stands near us, gives even inexperienced men the courage not to seek to avoid the inevitable. So the gladiator, who throughout the fight has been utterly faint-hearted, offers his throat to his opponent and even directs the wavering blade to the vital spot."[10]

Gladiators showed that even the lowest man could become good. By revealing their inner qualities of courage and discipline, they showed that even Rome's rigid social order could be inverted. The training that gladiators underwent could turn the most desperate criminal into a model of Romanness. Cicero was astonished at the contrast between the social backgrounds of gladiators and the strong characters they could reveal in the fights. "Just look at the gladiators, either debased men or foreigners, and see the blows they endure. See how they have been trained to accept a blow rather than avoid it like a coward." These men thought only of the happiness of their master and the people. Even when they were covered with wounds they still tried to please their master. And if they did please them then they were content to die. Their self-control was total. As Cicero goes on to say, "Even a mediocre gladiator never groans or changes the expression on his face. They never act shamefully, either standing up or falling down. And even when they do lose, they never shrink from offering their neck when ordered to receive the blow."[11]

Another piece of legal fiction underlines this contrast between the low status of the gladiator and the pillar of society that they could become. It involves the supposed case of a man who had signed on to become a gladiator in order to be able to afford to bury his father properly. He was led around on the day of the show with a placard describing his motivations. The people of the crowd were so impressed by this act of filial piety that they gave him the wooden sword of retirement before the fight had even started. Later he became so rich that he could enter the class of knights, the equestrians. He should now have been able to sit and enjoy the games from the rows near the front set aside for that class. But the law stated that anyone who had been a gladiator was barred from these seats. The question was, then, whether he had been a gladiator as he had not actually fought as one. The case for his defense emphasized how morally he had lived after his release: "How frugally he made his fortune, how parsimoniously, how laboriously! I would venture to say that no other knight or anyone else has done the like."[12]

If he fought bravely and skilfully, the gladiator was able to earn enough respect from the crowd that, despite his low status, he could be saved. Even the defeated, if they had fought like a man, could earn salvation. He became the living embodiment of the traditional Roman military virtues of bravery, manliness, and discipline that had made Rome the most successful society the world had ever seen. This was a powerfully transformative act for the crowd to witness. In the arena, before their eyes, the spectators saw some of the most worthless outcasts in society, men who were little better than slaves, change into models of traditional Roman virtue. No wonder the Christians felt so uneasy about this rival form of salvation. Those fighters who failed to take this opportunity to redeem themselves faced death. Rome, in its mercy, had offered them the chance to save themselves and if, through their cowardice, they had balked at what was required of them, then the crowd could not be expected to show them any sympathy.

When we read about what happened in the arena, it is hard for us to see beyond the violence. If we went back in time and watched a day's entertainment, we would be appalled and confused by the wholesale slaughter of so many fine animals in the morning. How many of us could stomach the lunchtime executions, when the screams of the victims resonated around the Colosseum? Perhaps we would have found the gladiatorial combats the easiest to watch. Like Augustine's friend, Alypius, I can imagine being taken along by the crowd's passion and finding it impossible not to follow the action before me. I like to think I would call for mercy for the defeated but for how long I cannot say.

But the Romans had a different attitude toward violence. Theirs was a brutal society. Perhaps over a third of the population of Rome were slaves, who belonged to their masters and were viewed as completely expendable. Many, perhaps most, of the better-off section of society who attended the games in the Colosseum owned slaves themselves. They would have seen them flogged as punishment, seen them tortured in the law courts, where it was compulsory for a slave's testimony to be taken in this way, and have been brought up from early childhood to order slaves to follow their commands. Criminals were treated with gruesome cruelty, with the lowest being subject to a particularly slow and public execution in the form of crucifixion. One writer describes how rich Roman dinner parties might include two or three pairs of gladiators fighting before the couches: "when they have finished dining and are fueled with drink, they call in the gladiators. As soon as one has his throat cut, the diners applaud with delight."[13] These were not on the whole a people who were squeamish about violence.

Preindustrial societies commonly resorted to public displays of the most shocking violence to maintain law and order. It was a normal part of the criminal justice system. In part this reflected the harshness of normal life for most people, but it also stemmed from the very basic level of policing. The Roman legal system, for all its impressive achievements, was only ever able to prosecute and punish a tiny fraction of the criminals that operated within Roman society. Vivid, violent, and dramatic statements that publicly affirmed social norms sent out a powerful symbolic message to society as a whole. It was the execution of the deviant for the enjoyment of the decent. The execution-as-entertainment, therefore, represented much more than the expression of a sadistic psychopathology. Rome was a society where brutality was built into the system. In such a male-dominated, militaristic, hierarchical society, violence was the perfectly appropriate medium for the importance of order to be hammered home.

The violence of the arena was not the primary focus for the Roman audience. Violence was only perceived as shocking if it was inappropriate to the status of the individual on whom it was being afflicted. Instead, the blood and gore were incidental to what really mattered. The really important message was the network of shared assumptions about their collective Romanness that these violent games articulated in a physical form. It heralded the character traits that were the Romans' unique selling points: their honor, their desire for glory, their military prowess, their manliness. This is not to say that the Romans did not notice the violence. Death, wounds and aggression were what gave the games their piquancy. The Romans enjoyed violence because violence was the language of their power itself. The violent acts of the arena effectively dramatized the importance of certain fundamental social ideals. It might seem strange that violence became an obsession in an ordered society, but it reflected the force that maintained that order itself.

Similarly, death was important but it wasn't the be-and-end-all of the gladiatorial combats. Death certainly provided valuable lessons to the viewer. But defeated gladiators did not always die. We have seen that in almost all the records of combat uncovered in Pompeii, the defeated gladiator was granted mercy. Many gladiators were spared on multiple occasions, particularly once they had become favorites with the crowd. Instead, what seems to have been the focus for the Roman spectator were the style, bravery, and skill of the combatant, rather in the way that aficionados of bullfighting concentrate on the courage and grace of the matador rather than the kill itself.

Graceful aggression was the medium through which the meanings of the games were articulated. The studied control and meticulous comportment gave the games an undeniable elegance. Cicero describes how "boxers, and gladiators not much less, do not make any motion, either in cautious parrying or vigorous thrusting, which does not have a certain grace, so that whatever is useful for the combat is also attractive to look upon."[14] Quintilian describes how gladiators and wrestlers who rely solely on their strength are usually undone by their opponents' simple skill: "it is of frequent occurrence in such cases for the latter to be overthrown by his own strength and the former to find the fury of his onslaught parried by his adversary with a simple turn of the wrist."[15] Similarly, in the Circus the charioteer was expected to be an expert strategist. Pliny the Elder describes how after a charioteer of the white faction was thrown at the start, "his team took the lead and kept it by obstructing their rivals, jostling them aside and doing everything against them that they would have had to do with a most skillful charioteer in control."[16] Above all, we have seen that in the arena the proper conventions also had to be observed in death. The gladiator was expected to die in the correct position, with chest out, leaning to the right, head drooping, half-seated on his weapons. A gladiator learned in his training school how to "accept the sword" and receive the blow "with his whole body." This was the dying swan of the Roman world; a formalized, stylized way of death.

The crowd harbored no guilt about what happened to the victims. They were extremely critical of any performance that did not come up to the mark. The people called out for a defeated gladiator to expose his breast to receive a final blow. He must not flinch or draw back from the sword. Such cool, calm, and collected violence was what the Roman audience went to see. We find it hard not to see this simply as a kind of pathology, since the modern Western world tends to see most forms of violence in moral terms. But the crowd at the games saw the combination of grace, control, and aggression, when done well, as both beautiful and virtuous. The image of death became a cultural obsession, but the brutality was not the focus for the individual spectator. Death served as the lens through which Roman society could see itself in an intensely concentrated form. It was the medium not the message itself.

The games presented the audience with a self-image where the traditional military virtues stood out prominently. But the games had not existed in traditional Roman society. They took place in the urban centers of a sprawling empire, which had conquered most of its enemies and enjoyed power on a hitherto unimagined scale. The kind of manliness that the games sought to exalt was a contemporary take on these traditional virtues. In the same way, the animal hunts were an urban reexpression of the old hunts of the countryside in a way that made them meaningful for the masses and not just to a rural elite. It made no sense simply to assert that the Romans of imperial Rome were the same as the yeomen of yore who had fought in the legions of the republic. The nature of manliness had changed. Or at least, the ways in which a man was expected to express his virility had transformed from an agrarian and military setting to an urban civilian context.

Being a man in the imperial city of Rome demanded the same core qualities as it had always had. Men were expected to be aggressive and assertive, particularly in the public sphere. This image had traditionally been linked with military service. But by the time of the empire, as the legions became professionalized and were stationed away at the frontiers, this model of malehood became less relevant to the mass of the citizen body. Sport and combat in the Circus and Colosseum became the most prominent way for the traditional legionary's attributes of physical toughness, skill, and discipline to be reinterpreted in a more civilized format.

This new form of urban manliness was also portrayed as a corrective to many of Rome's prevailing social problems. The games encouraged manly pursuits and implicitly summoned women to their traditional roles in the household. Both were needed, because there was mounting concern among the political elite about the social conditions and moral welfare of the great mass of the urban poor in Rome. It is hard to understand how colossal Rome had become by the time of the empire. At a million strong, its inhabitants overwhelmed the traditional political structures and public spaces, such as the Forum. Most of these people were not tied in by any patronage links to the wealthy as might have been the case in smaller settlements. The small numbers of the elite, numbering somewhere between one and three percent of the population, depending on how they are defined, sat in a sea of urban poor who were not fully integrated into Roman society in the way that Roman citizens had been in the heyday of the republic.

That does not mean that there was fear of an imminent revolution. The popular politics was more concerned with the ever-present problems of trying to secure sufficient food and work to keep the wolf from the door. But it was clear that the old style of social relations had changed, which was highly unsettling in a world where change was not the norm and was treated with natural suspicion. Elite moralists looked at the urban living conditions of the tens of thousands who poured into Rome in search of a better life and could not but be fearful of the effects on their physical and psychological condition. The strong farmers who had won Rome its greatness were being replaced by what could be seen as a lazy, undernourished, and morally corrupt mass, whose main concern was not the acquisition of glory but bread and circuses.

The games were a way to address some of these elite concerns. Gladiators were impressive physical specimens who fought to win the glory that the Roman people had in their power to grant them. Their achievements were proof that men had not become soft and that the social order would not come apart as a result of the changes that had occurred. They showed that even the worst kind of individuals could be changed by the transformative power of Roman habits. But the success of gladiators also served as a warning. If anyone could become Roman-like in their military skills, then the Romans had better watch out. Rome needed to maintain its military traditions or else it risked slipping into a moral and physical decay that could only have one result: defeat.

The games epitomized what was best about the Roman male, at least in their own eyes. The games symbolized the Roman struggle and ultimate victory. In them, the crowd saw shining examples of individuals suffering for the benefit of the wider community. But the games also served as an ongoing reenactment of how the Romans needed to behave if they were to maintain that success. The chaos of the late republic, a time marked by a series of uprisings and civil wars, had left Roman society striving to find a new set of directions for itself. The empire needed a common destiny. It needed to disown the dreadful mess of the recent past. It needed a new sense of moral purpose. Building on the political role that the games had acquired under the republic, the emperors used the games to establish a new form of Roman identity. Future generations were to experience the thrill of victory, and, in the model society that was drawn up to watch this spectacle, a fantastical representation of social relations was produced to reflect a return of the golden age. The games increased in popularity with the advent of empire. Increasing amounts of resources were directed toward them, because such entertainments played such a fundamental role in the imperial settlement that brought an end to the troubles of the late republic. Indeed, their spectacular decadence has meant that the games have become a byword for the Roman Empire itself.

The rituals of the spectacles expressed the aspirations of the imperial government in a dramatic form. The emperors wanted to be leaders of a well-ordered, disciplined society that knew how to use its leisure properly. The vicious punishments meted out to the condemned publicly reaffirmed these social ideals. Paradoxically the games were also a means for the emperors to express their dominance over Roman society. Public entertainments provided opportunities for emperors to ignore society's moral norms with impunity. So, when Nero performed in the theater or Commodus "fought" as a gladiator, it showed that these supreme rulers were above the law. In such an environment, it is not surprising that the people mostly delivered the acclamations and applause that the emperors wanted, particularly in the amphitheater where the audience was more weighted toward those with a larger stake in Roman society.

But it would be a mistake to think that the imperial view of the games is the only possible take on things. The dominating figure of the emperor should itself make us careful about seeing the games as representing how all Romans thought. That would be accepting the imperial propaganda at face value and seeing the Roman world as the emperors presented it. The emperors placed a great burden on the games to win over the crowd and re-create the social harmony that had been lost in the discord of the late republic. In such a multicultural empire, the games also met a need for social unity, cohesion, and integration. The extraordinary expenditure on public entertainment throughout the Roman world was justified, because it provided a way for the empire to be bound together through the shared pursuit of pleasure. The spectacles created a cultural vocabulary that could unite the diverse peoples under Roman control. In other words, the games were key to bringing about Romanization. But other interpretations and attitudes toward the games existed that should prevent us from seeing them as a monolithic institution.

For one thing, there was significant local variation across the empire to adapt to local tastes. Gladiators seem to have been far less popular in North Africa, where the preference was for stand-alone animal hunts of the sort that the Magerius mosaic commemorates. We have to remember that we are reliant on scraps of evidence and so we are unable, as yet, to work out exactly how varied in format and detail the games were across the empire.

Another problem is that it is not clear that "Roman" always meant the same thing everywhere. The empire was so vast and diverse, including dozens of local languages and cultures, that "Roman" was never a stable category. The Romans never simply stamped their identity onto those they ruled. They always had to accommodate them in some ways, often by adopting some of their gods or exercising their authority through existing local elites. All of these subordinate groups were able to interpret the cultural performances of the arena in different ways. No doubt many bought in to the Roman system, but others, especially in minority groups such as the Christians, saw the games as the epitome of wickedness and symbols of all that was wrong about Roman rule.

So, even if we accept that the games created a focal point for Roman society in which it was able to articulate its own self-image and core values, we must realize that this was not simply rolled out across the Roman world. This was how the emperors wanted to see their world: neatly ordered and successful under their wise leadership. But games were held in different communities across the Roman world, sometimes in small and inconsequential places. Here the giver of the games acted as the emperor's representative, but it was a far cry from the political meeting between the emperor and the Roman people in the capital city. Provinces as far apart as Egypt, Pisidia in modern-day Turkey, Pannonia in what is now Eastern Europe, and Spain all had their own take the games. Different social groups also cannot be expected to have had the same opinion of what the games meant. Their interpretations will also have developed over the long life span of the empire. Sadly, we just do not have enough evidence to chart these variations with any certainty.

Even within Rome itself, we find that some people had problems with the games. We have already noted the moral concerns of some elite traditionalists. Some of this criticism of spectacles centered on its perceived impact on the viewer. Some elite writers complained of the damaging effect of spending time surrounded by the emotionally intense atmosphere of the crowd. It all smacked of a lower-class lack of self-control that could rub off on the restrained nobleman. This kind of moral opprobrium against the games as a form of popular entertainment focused especially on what the elite saw as time wasting. In the good old days, Cicero thought that the games were justified, because they gave viewers a graphic education in how to endure pain and death. This was just the kind of lesson that Roman citizens needed before they went off to fight in the legions. But by Cicero's day, when Rome had become full of inhabitants who would never set foot on a battlefield, watching the games had become a way for good-for-nothing layabouts to idle away a day.

This combination of leisure and vulgarity is what Seneca complains about most in his famous passage criticizing the midday executions.[17] Nothing is so damaging to good character, he argues, as the habit of lounging at the games. That is when vice steals upon you by means of pleasure. During the midday executions, when some of the victims were forced to fight to the death without any defensive armor, the danger of being corrupted in this way was at its peak. That was when the quality of the entertainment nosedived, according to Seneca. The dregs of the spectators who were left watching during this lull, when more respectable viewers had gone for lunch, demanded a similarly rough level of entertainment. The outcome of every fight was death and skill played no part. It was bad enough in the morning, when the crowd had shouted out "Kill him! Whip him! Burn him!" if a fighter showed any sign of cowardice. They complained if a gladiator refused to die enthusiastically. Even when the intermission started, there was just a little throat cutting to keep the few spectators still present entertained. Watching what he saw as the charmless vulgarity of this most brutal part of the games, left Seneca feeling greedy, more ambitious, more pleasure-seeking, and even more cruel and inhuman. In other words, it left him feeling like a vulgar plebeian. This kind of lack of sensibility was exactly what traditional upper-class Romans believed characterized the degenerate urban populace of their own day.

Seneca's view was a rarity, which was why he felt it worth recording at all. His outrage is directed not so much at the violence or cruelty that was inflicted on the victims—he accepts that criminals deserve to suffer a dreadful fate—but against the debilitating effects on the lower orders of such time wasting. What was even more important was that such an immoral atmosphere even seemed to have the power to corrupt the upper classes. If a man of Seneca's caliber could be tainted, then it was no surprise that other lesser members of the elite could be enticed to go so far as to actually appear in the games.

The end of the republic had seen a protracted and bloody civil war that had left deep wounds in Roman society. The huge size of the city of Rome meant that traditional forms of social relations, such as patron-client relationships, were less relevant. The great mass of the urban populace were not all recognizably Roman as had been the case in the early republic. Rome was full of immigrants and slaves who had come from all over the empire and beyond. Not many of the urban population could be described as "pure" Roman in the same way as some of the most aristocratic families could. The multicultural melting pot that was the great imperial city of Rome created a dire need for cultural focal points that could unite this disparate mass. The games were one such focal point.

The first emperor Augustus had sought to re-create Roman identity, based on traditional themes of piety, virtue, and loyalty. The emperor himself represented the epitome of these values and served as the cultural center for Roman society as a whole. The games were a place where this new identity and society were most clearly on view. Pleasure and politics were fused into a powerful alloy that overcame traditional objections to the non-elite having access to leisure and luxury. The games would not corrupt the people, it was argued, because they established imperial legitimacy, maintained social hierarchy, and created social consensus. In order to attract the people into this social contract, the emperors made the games appealing to popular tastes. They were sensational, spectacular, and simple to appreciate. This contrasted with refined elite tastes and so some, like Seneca, sneered at the vulgarity of the games.

But most of the elite seem to have been happy to buy into the new imperial culture along with everyone else. The many examples we find of nobles and well-born Romans volunteering to fight as gladiators underline just how acceptable it had become to do so, whatever old-fashioned critics like Seneca said. In the past, it would have been unthinkable for an aristocrat to want to appear on the stage or in the arena. The shame would have seen them ostracized by their peers. But with the emperors giving their support to the games, and the games being so popular, appearing as a performer was a natural act for those seeking to gain popularity and prestige. Only reactionaries like Seneca were left to complain.

The sources we have from these traditionalists did not reflect popular opinion. Augustus had recognized the urgent need to generate a more inclusive image of Romanness, which could appeal to a widely diverse set of urban individuals rather than a culturally homogeneous set of Roman yeomen. The games repackaged traditional Roman qualities into a format that was far more appropriate to the reality of the imperial city. These games drew on accepted Roman virtues and areas of shared knowledge, such as mythology, to try and create a new social consensus after the ruptures of the civil wars. The games of the arena represented a reinterpretation of military training and aristocratic hunting that would appeal to the lower classes.

The games broadcast an image of society that was well-ordered and cohesive. It proclaimed that Roman society was at peace with itself, celebrating its success and sharing its pleasures in the same uniform way. We can see the gladiator and the charioteer as role models for the Roman viewer: competitive, tough, but fully under the control of the patron of the games. But we should ask whether this view was in fact universally shared. Did everyone like to see the Romans as they did themselves? We have already seen some fleeting examples of resistance and opposition to the brutality of the games. The Christians who were martyred in the empire's arenas clearly did not share these Roman ideals. Some mainstream elite Roman writers had concerns about the moral and personal impact that being surrounded by a crowd of screaming plebeians could have. Many elite Romans did not believe that the poor either deserved such generous leisure provision or knew how to handle its potentially corrupting effects. They also sneered at some of the vulgarity and sensationalism. It is an irony that these concerns emanated from the very people who were often funding them.

These anxieties reveal that the games were not entirely unproblematic in Roman society. Not everyone simply bought in to the new type of identity that was on display in the arena. But there were also political concerns. The emperors needed to win over the people by giving the people what they wanted, in the form of cheap bread and entertainment. In doing so they risked alienating the aristocracy who saw themselves as more deserving targets of imperial patronage. The emperor needed to carry out a careful balancing act here. He had to apportion his support carefully among the classes. If the emperor was seen to be too generous to the crowd, as Commodus was, then he could expect to face a powerful elite backlash in the form of conspiracy, slander, and character assassination in the literature. Anecdotal stories about how such emperors behaved in the games, as when Commodus killed a rhinoceros, became an acceptable part of serious history, because they could be used as political weapons by Roman historians against emperors whose regimes they wanted to disparage.

If the games taught you how to be a Roman, then they also gave opportunities for some to reject this lesson. The games provided a powerful image of Roman unity, but they also revealed the social fissures that continued to exist in society. Different social groups were able to see the games in their own way, not simply as the emperors wished them to. It is tempting to see the games being held across the emperor as evidence for the widespread acceptance of Roman ideals. But it is impossible to say just how deeply this games culture penetrated the many different local cultures of the empire. We do know that some groups fought back hard against this attempt to railroad them into becoming more Roman.

Fighting Back

ON THE SEVENTH OF MARCH, AD 203, in the splendid amphitheater at Carthage, a city that had long since been subsumed into the Roman province of Africa, a twenty-two-year-old noblewoman, called Perpetua, was led out to be executed. She was the woman we encountered earlier who had recently given birth and whose breasts dripped with the milk she was still producing for her child. Accompanying her were a group of co-condemned friends. Their crime was to belong to that most hated of religious sects, the Christians. The packed crowd bayed for their blood. To appease them the governor had them whipped before a line of gladiators. Then a wild boar, a bear, and a leopard were unleashed on the men. Once that bloodbath was over, a wild cow was set on the women. Battered to a pulp by this beast, Perpetua was eventually put out of her misery by a gladiator. But even then her suffering did not stop. He was a novice, and his hand shook so much that he missed with his first blow and merely wounded her. Perpetua had to set the blade upon her own neck before he was able to kill her with a downward thrust.

What is remarkable about this story of Christian martyrdom is that we possess an eyewitness account of it. The text, *The Passion of St. Perpetua, St. Felicitas, and Their Companions*, tells how this small group of practicing Christians were arrested and imprisoned, before being condemned to death for refusing to renounce their faith. The group consisted of Perpetua, her pregnant slave Felicitas, another slave named Revocatus, and two free men called Saturninus and Secundulus. They were later joined voluntarily by another Christian called Saturus.

Even more remarkable is that the bulk of the account was almost certainly written by Perpetua herself. Only the introduction and the description of the martyrs' death in the arena were added later by an editor. This is not only an autobiographical telling of what it was like to be condemned to the beasts of the games, it is also a rare ancient text that was written by a woman. With its often highly charged and emotional narrative, it gives us a unique insight into the games and what it was like to be a victim.

Perpetua was married and had recently given birth to a boy. She came from a wealthy background but, despite her traditional education, had come into contact with Christianity. Both she and one of her two brothers had converted. It is hard to convey how shocking this would have been for her family. To take up Christianity was to renounce the gods. It was to reject the very divine powers who had made Rome the master of the world. It was to see the Lord as your father and your fellow believers as brothers and sisters in Christ, replacing your real siblings and family. A father was the law for most young Roman women. They were brought up to respect, revere, and obey him. To reject his authority was to reject one of the core institutions and bases of society.

This is why the account dwells so much on Perpetua's dialogues with her father. Her words open by referring to his anger at her for joining what was then seen as a crackpot religion. The two of them were constantly at loggerheads over her conversion, and he was always trying to persuade her to renounce her new faith and return to the old gods. But she would have none of it. "Do you see that pot over there?" she said, "Would you give it any other name?" And when he replied that he would not, she said, "So it is with me, for I am a Christian and cannot call myself anything else." Her father was furious and rushed at her as if to tear her eyes out before he stormed off.

Perpetua and her Christian companions had already been noticed by the authorities. Soon they were arrested and put into jail. She was terrified: "I had never known such darkness." It was stiflingly hot in the overcrowded room and the soldiers handled them roughly. Even worse was the fact that her newborn son had had to be left behind. She agonized about his feeding as she was still breastfeeding him.

Luckily, two of her Christian friends managed to bribe the guards so that Perpetua was taken out of the dungeon to a better part of the prison where she met with her family. Her mother had brought the infant with her, and Perpetua suckled her child that was now faint with hunger. Knowing what fate was likely to await her, Perpetua entrusted her son to her mother and brother. Seeing how grief-stricken they were, she too felt upset. For days she sat in the prison agonizing about leaving her child. In the end she managed to get permission to have the child live with her in the cell. Immediately her health improved and the prison seemed like a palace to her.

Her Christian brother was desperate to know whether she would be martyred or not so she asked God for a vision. That night she dreamed of a huge but narrow bronze ladder, which reached up as far as heaven. The sides of the ladder were covered with swords, spears, hooks, and knives, so that if anyone went up it they had to be careful to keep their gaze fixed straight ahead so that they were not slashed by the weaponry. At the bottom of the ladder lay a huge serpent, waiting to devour those who were too afraid to climb. Saturus was the first to climb and, when he had reached the top, he called down to Perpetua to follow. She ascended and saw a wide expanse of gardens, in the middle of which sat a man. His hair was white, he was dressed as a shepherd, and he was milking his sheep. Thousands stood around him. The man raised his head and said to Perpetua: "Welcome, child." He then gave her curd from the milk, which she ate, and all that stood about her said, "Amen." And at the sound of that word she woke up. Perpetua told the dream to her brother and they both then knew that she would die. They abandoned all hope of her being saved, in this world at least.

As their trial drew near, her father became utterly exhausted. He visited Perpetua and begged her to take pity on his gray hairs. "With these hands," he said, "I have raised you up to be such a beautiful young woman. Look on your family and your poor son, who will not live long after you, and do not be so resolved to die. Do not destroy us all together." He kissed her hands and groveled at her feet, weeping all the while. But Perpetua was implacable. To be sure she grieved for him, but she was dead set on following God's will.

Soon the group of Christians was brought to trial in the Forum. A great crowd of people came to watch. One by one the accused confessed to being Christians, even though Perpetua's father had another attempt at persuading her, holding her son before her to try to entice her away from her faith. Even Hilarion the judge joined in, appealing to her to have pity on her father. All she had to do was make a sacrifice to the true gods for the emperor's prosperity. "Have mercy on your child," the judge said to her.

"I am a Christian," was her firm response.

The judge condemned them all to be thrown to the beasts in the arena. Cheerfully they went back down to the dungeon. Perpetua sent for her child again, who had been staying with her family during the trial. But her father refused to hand the boy over. It was, she believed, only God's intervention that prevented her from being tormented by anxiety for the child and by the pain in her swollen breasts.

In the last days before her execution, Perpetua suffered further powerful dreams. She dreamed of her young brother Dinocrates, who had died of a facial cancer when only seven. In the last few days before the games, which were being held to celebrate the emperor's birthday, the condemned were transferred to a military prison. Perpetua prayed tearfully through the night that she would be reunited with her poor dead brother. As the day of the games drew near, her father had one last go. He plucked out the hairs of his beard and fell on his face begging her to pity him and change her mind. But it was to no avail.

The night before the games, Perpetua dreamed that she fought the devil himself in a gladiatorial combat. She had been led into the arena, where she was stripped naked and turned into a man. She was covered in oil as would normally be done before a contest. Against her came the devil. So big was he that he towered over the amphitheater itself. He wore a purple robe, as if he were a Roman emperor, and had shoes curiously wrought in gold and silver. He carried a rod like a master of gladiators.

They began to fight. They pummeled each other and he tried to trip her up. But Perpetua rose up high into the air and began to kick him in the face with her heels. She punched him to the ground and trod on his head. The people began to shout, and her supporters started to sing. Then she went up to collect her victory branch and headed toward the gate called the Gate of Life. She had triumphed.

Perpetua's firsthand account breaks off here. It was left to another to write the description of her fate in the arena the next day.

Her slave Felicitas had been condemned to the beasts but, because she was pregnant, in accordance with Roman law was to have been held back until she had given birth. The group of Christian friends had prayed that the baby would come early so that the mother could die alongside them. And their prayers were answered. Three days before the games, the birth pangs hit. As she cried out in agony, one of the jailers mocked her, saying that the pain was nothing compared with what she would suffer when she was thrown to the beasts. She gave birth to a daughter, whom a sister of hers brought up as her own. Felicitas was now free to join her friends in their fate.

The night before the games, the condemned were given their last supper. As was usual, local people came to watch this macabre event, mocking them for their stupidity at not sacrificing to the gods. The Christians threatened them with the judgment of the Lord and swore that they were delighted to be suffering martyrdom. And so on the following morning, the group left the prison and entered the amphitheater as if it were heaven. Their faces were cheerful and bright. If they trembled, it was out of joy not fear.

When they arrived at the gate, the men were forced to dress as if they were priests of Saturn, while the women were compelled to wear the clothing of priestesses of Ceres. Perpetua stood firm to the last and refused. This was why they were in this situation, after all, because they refused to renounce their faith. She was not about to change that at the very moment of her martyrdom. Even the Romans could see the justice in this, and so the tribune allowed them to be brought forward dressed as they were.

Perpetua began to sing. The male Christians Revocatus, Saturninus, and Saturus threatened the crowd as they stared down at them from the seats. Then when they came into sight of the judge Hilarion, they shouted at him: "You judge us but God will judge you!" The people were infuriated by this arrogance and called for the Christians to be whipped before the beast fighters. As they were flogged, the Christians gave thanks because they had shared some of Jesus's sufferings.

Saturninus had for a long time yearned to be thrown to the wild beasts and so prove his devotion to God. And, as God had made clear, ask and you shall receive. So at the beginning of the spectacle, Saturninus and Revocatus were to be confronted with a bear. They were to be tied to a raised platform in the middle of the arena where all the spectators could get a good view and be ripped to pieces by the beast. In contrast to Saturninus' bravura, Saturus dreaded nothing more than a bear. The attendants had actually already tried to tie him to a wild boar so that he would be slashed by its sharp tusks. But the animal keeper had himself been torn apart by the beast and died later as a result of his wounds. Saturus himself suffered nothing worse than being dragged about the sand by the animal, who otherwise left him alone. And when he had been tied to the platform as a plaything for the bear, the beast would not come out of his lair.

The spectacle culminated with the release of the leopard, always a favorite with the North African crowd. He attacked Saturus and bit him with such ferocity that he was instantly bathed in so much blood that the crowd shouted out, "Have a nice bath!" It was like a second baptism. As he lay slowly dying, the attendants came over to his prostrate body and dragged him off to the place outside the arena where half-dead victims were finished off by having their throats cut.

A particularly savage wild cow had been kept aside for the Christian women. They were stripped and put in nets, before being brought out into the arena. A frisson of shock, disgust, and excitement went round the crowd when they saw that one was a tender young girl and the other's breasts were still lactating from her recent childbirth. We have seen that this indecency was too much for the audience to bear. They demanded that the young women were taken out and clothed properly. Perpetua was the first to be thrown back into the arena. As she was knocked down by the beast, she fell and tore her new garment up the side. Modestly, she tried to pull the tear together in order to cover her thigh that had been revealed. She then searched for a pin to tie up her disheveled hair, so determined was she that she should meet her maker decently. By now, Felicitas had also been thrown in only to be knocked down. Perpetua stood up and went over to Felicitas and pulled her to her feet.

The crowd softened before this display of fine female modesty. They called for the pair to be brought back to the Gate of Life. When they reached there, Perpetua came to as if she had been in a trance. She looked about her and, to everyone's amazement, asked, "When are we to be thrown to the cow?" It was only when they showed her the cuts and bruises on her body that she believed them when they told her that it had already happened.

Then the people demanded that all the Christians who were still alive should be brought back and put to the sword before them. They wanted to witness the final slaughter of this troublesome bunch. Calmly the Christians got up and walked to their fates, kissing each other in a display of brotherly and sisterly love. Those who were so badly injured that they were incapable of moving received their death blows in silence. Perpetua was so steadfast that, as we have seen, she guided her inexperienced executioner's wandering hand and set his sword on her own neck.

How are we to understand these gruesome events? The first point we have to realize is that it was no accident that the Christians chose to challenge Rome in the arena. Martyrs were the most fanatical of Christians, determined that their actions should bear witness to the strength of their faith. The word *martyr* is itself Greek for a witness. By refusing to find any compromise with the Roman authorities, they ramped up the stakes until the Romans felt compelled to sentence them to death. In the same way that the terrorists of 9/11 sought two of the most prominent symbols of global capitalism for their attack, Christian martyrs sought to reject the powerful image of idealized Romanness that the arena created. It was precisely because the games served as a powerful assertion of what it meant to be Roman that Christians were happy to have their alternative vision of society displayed there. Where the Romans saw legitimacy and hierarchy, the Christians saw a massacre of the innocents.

But we should be careful not to take these accounts completely at face value. They are no doubt full of exaggerations and fabrications. Above all, we must remember that such persecutions were rare. The Romans were not always out to get the Christians, seeing them for the most part as a strange sect to be left alone to their own devices. Some periods of persecution were associated with the Roman state's suffering setbacks and looking for scapegoats, such as the Great Fire in AD 64 and the barbarian invasions of the mid-third century. These occasions were when Nero had Christians burned in Rome and Decius first launched a more systematic attempt to force Christians to pay homage to the Roman pantheon. Other persecutions seem to have been more associated with emperors' attempts to assert traditional religious mores as part of a wider program of reform, such as the Great Persecution of Diocletian. Marcus Aurelius simply seems to have been trying to keep the games supplied with victims when the plague had resulted in a shortage of manpower.

But year after year, there were no Christian martyrs. The Romans simply were not interested in them. Even when attempts were launched to try to force all members of the empire to sacrifice to the gods for the emperor's well-being, those who refused were, like Perpetua, given frequent opportunities to recant and so save themselves. The number who were actually thrown to the beasts was relatively small. We cannot know exactly how many, but the fact that it cannot be proved that any Christian was ever thrown to the lions in the Colosseum is testament to the rarity of such acts of persecution more generally.

We should also bear in mind that Rome was a relatively unsophisticated preindustrial society. It had no police force. Enforcing imperial decrees demanding universal sacrifice was an impossible task. It was probably quite easy to avoid persecution by leaving your home town and staying with friends or Christians elsewhere. Or you could go into hiding. Or get a pagan friend to sacrifice on your behalf (unless God would see that as cheating). Or buy a fake certificate saying that you had sacrificed. Or you could simply hex yourself and go ahead and sacrifice. Surely the Lord would know that you did not mean it?

If you steadfastly refused, you would find yourself being placed under all kinds of pressure. Like Perpetua, your family, above all your father, would lean on you to maintain the family reputation. This was not an easy force to resist. We can see accounts, such as that of Perpetua, as training manuals for would-be Christian martyrs. It warned them of what pressures they were likely to face and how they could overcome them. It taught them what to expect at every level of the process, even down to the final coup de grace. Above all it taught them how a good Christian should behave if he or she was to act as a shining beacon of the moral superiority of the Christian faith.

It was this direct challenge to the Roman way of life that the crowd found so outrageous and is no doubt the reason they were so hostile to this extreme approach of certain early Christians. In line with the picture of spectators as active and fully involved in what was being played out before them, we find the crowd commenting on and influencing the mechanics of the martyrs' torment and execution at every stage. It is to satisfy them that the tribune had the Christians flogged, dressed, and brought back for execution. The bravery of the Christians seemed to annoy the audience, particularly when the victims started to threaten the tribune himself with future punishment at the hands of their God. When another Christian, called Attalus, was martyred in Lyon during the summer of AD 177, the crowd were particularly keen to see him killed because he was man of some status. He was led round the amphitheater, preceded by a placard on which was written, "This is Attalus the Christian," and the people swelled with indignation against him. But the people did not always get what they wanted. The governor discovered that Attalus was a Roman citizen and so ordered that he was taken back to prison and for his case to be referred to a higher authority.

Perhaps the Romans liked their victims to beg and plead for mercy and to be cowardly in a way that reflected their worthlessness. It is clear that they saw these Christians as extremists who were completely deserving of their fate. This was justice in action. But the crowd also seems capable of respecting the victims when they behaved with a courage and modesty that would befit the most Roman of Roman fighters. They do not completely ignore the sufferings of the victims, but see these as a legitimate result of the Christians' fanatical opposition to the Roman gods.

The support of the pagan gods was what the crowd believed brought them security and prosperity. All that the Romans demanded of the Christians was that they make a simple gesture of worship to their traditional gods. Why was this too much to ask? The average pagan Roman in the crowd seems to have found it utterly incomprehensible that anyone would so pigheadedly throw away their life simply to make a point. What made the crowd so furious was that the refusal of a few crazy Christians to honor the gods risked the whole community's well-being. That is why their open extremism demanded a public, communal punishment.

If Christian victims still refused to recant when placed under the full torment and torture of the law, then this infuriated the audience even more. Origen describes how Roman magistrates were extremely angry when victims of torture bore their sufferings with great fortitude.[1] By contrast, they loved it when a Christian did give in. The stubborn refusal of those who would not served merely to underline how intransigent and opposed Christians were seen as being to the Roman lifestyle. So those who died for their faith could be further dishonored by having their bodies left unburied. The Romans believed this would deny them their hoped-for physical resurrection. The whole process of punishment in the arena, from being ripped apart and eaten by beasts to being burned alive, effectively destroyed all physical traces of these social outcasts.

The Romans felt obliged to reassert their loyalty to their gods by punishing the Christians, but, again, it is worth remembering that only occasionally did they do so. Such total resistance to the ideals of Romanness was rare. It was only these rigorous Christian martyrs who were prepared to challenge this society openly, and they paid a high price for doing so. We should not doubt that to a large extent the games did their job and made most people feel grateful for living in a peaceful and prosperous society under a beneficent emperor. But the fate of the Christians should also alert us to the fact that not everyone agreed with the ideology of the games. We have already seen occasions when ordinary people and participants did not consume or participate in the games in the way that was intended. They too could subvert the meanings of the games, even if they mostly did so in a far less dramatic way than the Christian martyrs did.

We find one example of such resistance, which was in fact a true piece of high drama. It was an occasion when a group of convicts, who had been condemned to fight in the games, were assigned to appear in the emperor Claudius's great sea battle, which he was re-creating on a lake. Seating was erected around the shores so that a huge crowd could come and watch this extravagant entertainment. Each side had twelve or fifty ships, depending on which source you believe, but before the battle commenced all the combatants were brought together before the emperor. "Hail, emperor, we who are about to die salute you," they cried, in what is the only known utterance of this phrase. To which Claudius replied, "Or not." It is unclear what he meant, probably that their salutes were not done with any conviction or sincerity, just as an attempt to curry favor with the emperor in the hope of getting him to let them off. But the fighters interpreted it as meaning that they would not die. In other words, the emperor had pardoned them and so they were free to go. They then refused to fight.

Claudius hesitated about whether he should simply have them all killed or not. But not wishing to disappoint the assembled throng, he eventually jumped up from his throne and ran along the edge of the lake, as best as his limp would allow, and, with a combination of threats and promises, he managed to persuade them to fight. The start of the battle was signaled by a horn born on a silver statue of a Triton, which emerged from the middle of the lake thanks to some mechanical device. Even then, when ordered to fight, they simply sailed through their opponent's lines of ships, injuring each other as little as possible. This continued until they were forced to destroy one another.[2]

Another striking example of participant resistance is found much later in the letters of Symmachus. He had assembled twenty-nine Saxon prisoners for the games he was putting on, but the night before they were due to appear, they strangled each other in their cell. We have already encountered another suicide to escape the horrors of the arena when a barbarian captive choked himself to death by forcing a toilet stick down his throat. "What a brave man," says Seneca, who records this story, and adds that it was a pity that such a courageous man did not make it to the arena, because he would have put up a great fight.[3]

These acts of resistance were as striking as they were rare. Most gladiators could only try to resist the dehumanization of the games in minor ways. They did this by forging close links with other fighters in their troupe. The gladiator's *familia* acted as his support network and it must have been one of the worst outcomes if two from the same group were paired against each other in a fight. We can only imagine what it was like to have to fight and then slaughter a close comrade. Their disciplined training allowed them to overcome it. The camaraderie among gladiators, at least among those who lived long enough to forge such relationships, is reflected in the tombstones that they sometimes erected for each other. "Loved by everyone" says one, "Avenged by my comrades" another. One gladiator is commended for having "Spared many lives" although it is not clear how he influenced the decision of the host. Perhaps he chose to merely wounded his opponents when he could have delivered a fatal blow. Some tombs seek to protect the reputation of fellow *familia* members, blaming another's cheating or the Fates for their death. They seem to have shared the crowd's desire for a fair fight. It is noticeable that they do not blame the crowd or the host for their demise.

The sense of camaraderie meant that a gladiator watched a fight from a very different perspective than that of the crowd. In the fictional "Case of the Ransomed Gladiator," when the rich man's son has to watch his poor friend fight in his place, we fight him full of anxiety and concern for his fate: "How apprehensively I watched!" His heart raced and he mirrored his friend's every move with his own body, ducking the blade when it was lifted threateningly, as if he himself was the target. "How agonizing was my concern for him!" he bemoans, "How relentless was the nature of my fear!"

Gladiators were not all the heartless murderers and cutthroats they were often made out to be. An account of the last meal on the evening before the fight describes how they are not all "entirely bestial." Even though fine food was put before them, some of the gladiators found greater pleasure in sorting out their last wishes. They would ask their friends to look after their wives if they didn't make it out alive, or they would set their slaves free. This was no time for a feast.[4] Thankfully a lucky few not only survived but even secured their freedom. One of these attests to his happy married life in his tombstone for his dead wife: "To the departed spirits of Maria Thisidis. Publius Aelius, a veteran Thracian gladiator from the Troad, put up this tombstone for his most holy, most devoted, well-deserving wife."[5] What must it have been like to be a gladiator's partner or child? The fear, the terror at every cheer ringing out from the arena, the financial uncertainties of losing the breadwinner must have been overwhelming.

We saw in chapter 5 that the audience was actively able to interpret events in the games in ways that were at odds with the intended message. They were as a group sophisticated and critical consumers who could do things their own way. The crowd seems sometimes to have ignored the seating and dress codes, as is evidenced by various imperial attempts to enforce them. The people of the crowd scratched graffiti into the seating as a way of reclaiming this grand architecture for themselves and their own messages. The seats in the amphitheater in Aphrodisias in Turkey, for example, were littered with gambling boards, phalluses, and abuse: "Bad years for the Greens," says one. Perhaps the gaming boards were for the intervals between fights or perhaps they were for the boring bits, when some spectators couldn't be bothered to watch the entertainment. It shows that there could be more than one way to watch the games as a spectator, not simply as a sponge soaking up the imperial propaganda. Sometimes there also seems to be unofficial humor implanted in the performance. The Magerius mosaic shows a leopard called "Romanus" being speared by a hunter; was this a little North African joke at the expense of their foreign masters?

One elite Roman writer sought to undercut the imperial message of these grand imperial events. The poet Ovid wrote during the time of Augustus, a period when the first emperor was attempting the moral reform of Roman society. In a back-to-basics series of laws, he promoted family life and condemned adultery, even going so far as to exile his own daughter Julia for her multiple affairs. Against this backdrop, Ovid wrote his poem "The Art of Love" (*Ars amatoria*), an instructional text on how to conduct relationships between men and women, not necessarily married. One of his recommendations was to take your lady to the Circus where you could squeeze up next to her and brush pretend bits of fluff from her chest. This blatant subversion of Augustus's attempts at moral reform probably contributed to his being later exiled to the miserable Black Sea town of Tomis.

Whether this kind of small-scale resistance ever amounted to much is impossible to say. It was certainly of a different order from that of the Christian martyrs. But even if most Christians opposed the ideology of the games, by far the majority of them did not express their opposition in the radical form of martyrdom. Instead they wrote texts condemning the games in the hope of converting Romans toward their new religion and also to prevent Christians from falling under the games' influence. The sheer quantity of Christian texts that attack the games just emphasizes how important a role the games played in mainstream Roman culture. They represented a vital target for the Christians to attack if they were to change society itself.

One means of doing so was to damn the games for their sensuousness. The five senses acted, the Christians argued, like open windows that gave access to the soul.[6] If anyone delighted in the pleasures of the Circus, or the struggles of athletes, or the versatility of actors, their soul risked being ensnared by the devil. Christian authors also saw the games as insane. Augustine thought it crazy that men were prepared to spend such vast sums on providing actors, beast fighters, and charioteers when there were poor to be fed. "They are all mad," he said, "the performers, the spectators, and the host."[7] Above all, the Christians criticized the games for being inhumane. It was horrific, they argued, that a man could be slaughtered for another's pleasure. Crime was not only committed, but it was taught, with training enabling men to have the power to murder in the arena. "What," says the early Christian bishop Cyprian, "can be said more inhuman or more repulsive?"[8]

One feature of the games that the Christians also disliked was their sexual atmosphere. Tertullian argued in the second century AD that Christians should not go to the theater, because that was the "home of immodesty" and was completely disreputable.[9] He was outraged by the lewd gestures and cross-dressing of popular Roman farces and the appearance of prostitutes on stage. He was astonished at the way men who were seemingly decent in normal life would transform in the games into not much more than animals. A man who would be too embarrassed to urinate in public would strip off in the Circus. A father who carefully protected his virgin daughter's ears from any bad language would take her to the theater where people swear like troopers. A quiet peace-loving man, who was shocked to see a corpse in normal life, would stare intently at the mangled and bloodied corpses of the arena. It was completely paradoxical, Tertullian argued, to have killers executed for their crimes but then reward gladiators with their freedom for killing them.

Opposition to such a central Roman institution as the games was an important way for the Christians to construct a new form of social identity. Christian identity partly involved inverting Roman assumptions about violence, hierarchy, and honor. They believed that they were missionaries for God's will and that he did not approve of the games. The fifth-century writer Orosius even argued that the collapse of the amphitheater at Fidenae in AD 27 should have been interpreted as a lesson in what happens to those who liked to witness the slaughter of their fellow men in gladiatorial combat.[10] But there was not complete disagreement between the Christians and the Romans about the games. They agreed that the guilty needed to be punished, just not in so brutal a manner. Some Christians were not out to resist the law but rather to reform it. John Chrysostom argued that law-abiding behavior would be increased if the games were banned, because they encouraged all kinds of violence and arguments in the cities. "For youth," he says, "when it has joined hands with idleness, and is brought up surrounded by such great evils as the games, becomes fiercer than any wild beast." And he tells an anecdote about how some barbarians once heard of the games and the extreme pleasure that the Romans took in them. "The Romans must have devised these pleasures," they said, "so they could behave as if they didn't have wives and children." It was all, in Christian eyes, just so much juvenile fun—but fun that was violent and had got out of hand. The Romans needed to grow up.[11]

In reality many ordinary Christians also enjoyed going to the games, especially the less violent shows in the theater and the Circus. We can see the virulent attacks on the shows by Christian writers as attempts to impose their radical new view of society on the many normal Christians for whom such entertainments were a routine part of life. It was not obvious to many Christians why the theater or Circus were such bad things and they remained popular well into the Christian empire. After the emperor Constantine's conversion to Christianity in AD 312, the Circus steadily replaced the amphitheater at the heart of the political relationship between the emperor and his people. It was no accident that, when Constantine founded his new Christian capital city at Constantinople, that the Circus sat at its heart, right next to the imperial palace.

One interesting example of Christians taking part in the chariot racing is the story of Italicus, who lived in Gaza. A Christian who held office in the town, he kept some racehorses so that he could compete against a rival pagan official who also kept horses. This rival used a magician to incite his horses with certain devilish incantations. He also used spells to curse Italicus's team. Worried about this, Italicus went to the Christian holy man, Hilarion, and asked for his help in protecting himself and his team against this kind of sorcery. Hilarion had no interest in wasting his time on such worthless trifles and told Italicus to sell the horses and give the money to the poor. Italicus replied that it was a duty of his office to provide horses for the games. And, he said, it would surely be better for the Christian horses to win than the pagan team. So Hilarion helped him and had holy water sprinkled on the horses, the charioteer and his chariot, and even on the course to protect the Christian team from diabolical interference.

On the day of the race, the crowd was in a state of extreme excitement, with both sides confident of victory. The signal to start was given: one team sped ahead, but the other stuck close to it. The wheels grew hot, and the shouts of the crowd swelled to a roar. And in a dramatic finale the pagan team was defeated by that of the Christian God. In their rage, the pagan audience demanded that Hilarion should be executed as a Christian magician. But this decisive victory, and several others that followed in successive games, were said to have caused many to convert to Christianity.[12]

The games were too deeply rooted in Roman culture for them to have been completely rejected by all Christians in practice. Even the accounts of the Christian martyrs strikingly reveal just how profoundly internalized were the ideals of the games. If we look closely at the Christian texts written to praise their heroic deaths, we find that these martyrs are portrayed as behaving exactly like good gladiators. In Perpetua's dream of the fight with the devil, for example, she won as a good gladiator would. Martyrs were praised for their courage and stamina. The martyr Blandina, despite being a weak woman, is described by Eusebius as "defeating her opponent the Devil in bout after bout and so won the crown of immortality."

Martyrs are portrayed as being phenomenally tough—able to withstand the harshest treatment. The account of the death of the bishop of Smyrna, Polycarp, in AD 155, describes how he and the other Christian victims were so torn with scourges that the frames of their bodies and even their veins and arteries were left open to see, but still they endured their suffering patiently. Their fortitude was so great that not a single groan escaped from them. Similarly, when Blandina and Attalus were killed, their companions endured every form

Maturus , Sanctus , Blandina , en eenen Jongeling uyt Pontius,
aen den waterstroom Rhone, seer jammerlijk gemartelifeerr,
ontrent Anno 172.

Seventeenth-century engraving showing the Christian martyrdom of Blandina in AD 177

of torture in the amphitheater. They were likened to athletes who were competing for the crown itself. The people of the crowd were so maddened by their endurance that they called for all kinds of torments. In the end, the martyrs were
placed in a red-hot iron chair, on which their bodies were roasted. Even that had
no effect. After the rest had been finished off, Blandina was the last to go, an end
to which she hastened with joy and exultation, much to the crowd's fury. After
she had been whipped, exposed to the wild beasts, and cooked in the chair, she
was finally put in a net and thrown before a bull. The bull tossed her about like a
toy, but she felt nothing. And once she too had been given the coup de grace,
even the heathen crowd had to admit that they had never seen a tougher woman.
In the end, the Christians had withstood their ordeal for so long that they
spoiled the day's fun for the crowd, because it meant that there was insufficient
time left for all the various entertainments that usually took place during gladiatorial shows.

In their graphic accounts of brutal martyrdom, Christian texts such as these took over the pagan ideals of the games and subverted them for their own ends. The Christians become the true victors, who outdid even the toughest gladiator in their virtue. But, in doing so, the Christians showed how internalized the language of the games had become in Roman society. Even the Christians needed the grammar of the games to express their own defiance to it. They could not escape this totalizing institution of the Roman world.

The Christian goal was to end the inhumane treatment and waste of life of the arena games and establish a society in which each individual had an opportunity to gain eternal salvation through his or her own unique relationship with God. In the end they were successful in having the gladiatorial contests banned, but it was not until AD 404 that it happened, almost a century after Constantine's conversion. The final straw had come when the emperor Honorius saw a monk called Telemachus enter the arena in an attempt to stop the fighting. The people of the crowd were so angry that they stoned him to death. Always hostile to the Christians, the historian Edward Gibbon dryly comments that his death was more useful to mankind than his life.[13]

The Christian tradition in combination with the sneering elitism of Roman writers like Seneca and Juvenal has skewed our view of the games. The image has been one of megalomaniac emperors, such as Commodus, providing decadent and dehumanizing spectacles to manipulate the Roman mob. This view has often been peddled by epic, and often not very accurate, movies and novels which have used selected ancient sources to appeal to these Judeo-Christian biases. Condescending viewers and readers alike have enjoyed these condemnations of pagans and perverted Romans, preferring to cheer on Western-style heroic and defiant rebels. The film *Gladiator* was but the latest in a long line of these portrayals. The effect of all this has been to reduce a multifaceted phenomenon to simple brutality, stupidity, and immorality. The games were far more than that. Trying to understanding why Commodus thought it was a good idea to kill a rhino can help us see just how complex and important an institution the games really were in the Roman world.

ACKNOWLEDGMENTS

This book aims to provide an up-to-date and graphic analysis of the Roman games for a general and introductory audience. It tries to give a modern, nonjudgmental presentation of this important topic from the emperors at the top to the lowest performers and spectators. The work I have contributed to the subject of the Roman games is spread around several specialist volumes and I wanted to present it in a more unified, accessible format. I also wanted to develop a number of new ideas I have had on the subject, which will, I hope, make this volume also of interest to a more academic audience.

The book generated a number of debts that I am pleased to have the chance to repay in some small way. The Master and Fellows of Churchill College, Cambridge, provided me with a wonderfully stimulating environment in which to write the text. Greg Aldrete fired my interest in the project by kindly inviting me to submit a proposal for the series. My editor at Johns Hopkins University Press, Matt McAdam, expertly steered the project through to completion, and his anonymous readers helped me tighten up the manuscript. My friends and colleagues Mary Beard, Peter Garnsey, Jon Gifford, Jason Goddard, Tessa Grant, Chris Hartley, Peter Harvey, Chris Kelly, Miranda Perry, Andrew Taylor, and Emma Widdis all helped with their usual support and encouragement. My wife, Anne, and son, Arthur, kept me grounded in the modern world. Above all, I want to thank Pierre Caquet, who acted as a convivial sounding board for many ideas during the writing of the book and to whom it is dedicated in thanks.

NOTES

PROLOGUE: THE RHINO DIES

1. M. Grant, *Gladiators* (London: Weidenfeld & Nicolson, 1967), pp. 124 and 128.
2. Seneca *Letters* 95.33 *satisque spectaculi*.

CHAPTER I: COMMODUS'S GREAT GAMES

1. Dio Cassius *Roman History* 66.25.1–5 describes the games of Titus and 77.1 describes the games of Septimius Severus in 202 AD.
2. Pliny the Elder *Natural Histories* 35.22 mentions walls in public porticoes covered with "lifelike portraits of all the gladiators" in a particular show.
3. Seneca *Letters* 7 describes the midday executions when the amphitheater was half-empty. Mosaics from Zliten picture condemned prisoners being wheeled out to be mauled by large cats.
4. Seneca *Letters* 70.20.
5. Pseudo-Quintilian *Declamations* 9, "The Case of the Ransomed Gladiator."
6. Seneca *On Providence* 3.4 describes how "the gladiator judges it ignominious to be set against an inferior, as he knows it is without glory to defeat one who can be defeated without danger."

CHAPTER III: AN EMPEROR LOVES HIS PEOPLE

1. Suetonius *Julius Caesar* 10.
2. Fronto *Letters* 2.18.9–17. Compare Juvenal's famous complaint that all the people of Rome want is now bread and circuses, *Satires* 10.77–81.
3. Augustus *My Achievements* 22–23.
4. Cicero *Letters to Atticus* 1.16.11, 2.19.3, 14.2; *Sestius* 54ff.
5. *Lives of the Later Caesars* Marcus Aurelius 29.
6. Tacitus describes the Circus and the theaters as the places for seditious whispers (*seditiosis vocibus*).
7. Lactantius *On How the Persecutors Died* 44.
8. Suetonius *Titus* 8.
9. Dio Cassius *Roman History* 60.28.
10. Suetonius *Tiberius* 45.
11. Dio Cassius *Roman History* 69.6.
12. Cicero *Sestius* 115.
13. Tacitus *Annals* 14.15 and 16.5.

14. Dio Cassius *Roman History* 59.13.
15. Dio Cassius *Roman History* 59.14.
16. Eusebius *History of the Church* 8.13.9.

CHAPTER IV: FEEDING THE MONSTER

1. Symmachus *Letters* 6.43.
2. *Papyrus Oxyrhynchus* 2707.
3. Polybius *Histories* 31.28; Martial *Epigrams* 10.41; Petronius *Satyricon* 45.
4. See, for example, Suetonius *Tiberius* 7 and 34.
5. Gaius *Institutes* 3.146.
6. *Corpus Inscriptionum Latinarum* 2.6278.
7. Ibid. 4.62. Tacitus gives the casualties as fifty thousand dead or maimed, Suetonius *Tiberius* 40 as over twenty thousand dead.
8. Dio Cassius *Roman History* 49.43.
9. Ammianus Marcellinus *History* 17.4.13.
10. See *Lives of the Later Caesars* Hadrian 18 and Justinian *Digest* 48.8.11.1–2.
11. Josephus *The War against the Jews* 6.418; 7.37–40.
12. Justinian *Digest* 48.19.31; Philostratus *Life of Apollonius of Tyana* 4.22.
13. Suetonius *Caligula* 27; Dio Cassius *Roman History* 59.10.
14. Suetonius *Julius Caesar* 26.
15. Petronius *Satyricon* 117; Seneca *Moral Letters* 37.1.
16. Tacitus *Histories* 2.62.
17. Tacitus *Annals* 15.32.
18. Justinian *Digest* 3.1.1.6.
19. See, for example, Tertullian *On the Spectacles* 22.
20. Dio Cassius *Roman History* 66.25; 67.8; Martial *On the Spectacles* 8.
21. Juvenal *Satires* 6.252ff.
22. Tacitus *Annals* 15.32; Dio Cassius *Roman History* 61.17.
23. On the various laws, see Dio Cassius *Roman History* 43.23, 48.43, 54.2, 56.25, 59.10, 76.16; Suetonius *Augustus* 39 and 43.
24. Quintilian *Institutes of Oratory* 5.13.54; Cicero *The Orator* 228.
25. Vegetius *Concerning Military Matters* 1.11.
26. Galen *Exhortation to the Study of the Arts*. See also Tatian *Address to the Greeks* 23.
27. John Chrysostom *Homily VIII on 1 Timothy ii.* 8–10; Tertullian *Against Heresies* 2.
28. Augustine *Tractate* 33.8; John Chrysostom *Homily 12 on Romans* 6.19.
29. Augustine *On the Trinity* 4.
30. Cyprian *On the Spectacles* 5.
31. *Corpus Inscriptionum Latinarum* 14.2884.
32. Juvenal *Satires* 7.114.
33. Ammianus Marcellinus *History* 26.3.3.
34. [Sulpicius Severus] *Letters* 6.
35. Augustine *Confessions* 6.8; *Psalm* 147.19.

CHAPTER V: WIN THE CROWD

1. Arnobius *Against the Pagans* 4.35.
2. Plutarch *Sulla* 35.

3. Dio Chrysostom *Orations* 32.77.

4. Josephus *Antiquities of the Jews* 19.24; P. J. J. Vanderbroeck, *Popular Leadership and Collective Behavior in the Late Roman Republic (ca. 80–50 B.C.)* (Amsterdam: J. C. Gieben, 1987) p. 152.

5. Dio Cassius *Roman History* 60.6.4–5; Arnobius *Against the Pagans* 4.31.

6. Ammianus Marcellinus *History* 28.4.

7. See, for example, Cyprian *On the Spectacles* 5.

8. Tertullian *On the Spectacles* 16.

9. *Lives of the Later Caesars* Commodus 15.

10. Justinian *Digest* 48.19.28.3

11. Tacitus *Annals* 14.17

12. Ammianus Marcellinus *History* 28.4.28–31.

13. Tertullian *On the Spectacles* 15–16.

14. Ammianus Marcellinus *History* 28.4.28.

15. Seneca *Letters* 1.7.

16. Martial *On the Spectacles* 9.

17. *Anthologia Latina* 415.27–28.

18. Pliny the Elder *Natural Histories* 8.20–1.

19. Pseudo-Quintilian *Declamations* 9 "The Case of the Ransomed Gladiator," 16.

20. Suetonius *Caligula* 55; Dio Cassius *Roman History* 63.6.

21. Cassiodorus *Letters* 3.51.11–12.

22. Procopius *History of the Wars* 1.24.1ff.

23. Quoted by H. S. Versnel in "Punish Those Who Rejoice in Our Misery: On Curse Tablets and Schadenfreude," in D. R. Jordan, H. Montgomery, and E. Thomassen (eds.), *The World of Ancient Magic* (Bergen: Norwegian Institute at Athens, 1999) pp. 125–62, p. 128.

24. Basil the Great *Letters* 221.

25. Cassiodorus *Letters* 51.

26. Tacitus *A Dialogue on Oratory* 29; Pliny the Younger *Letters* 9.6.

27. Cicero *Letters to Friends* 7.3.

28. Cyprian *On the Spectacles* 6.

29. Augustine *City of God* 2.4.

30. Marcus Aurelius *Meditations* 6.46

CHAPTER VI: How to Be a Roman

1. Aulus Gellius *Attic Nights* 6.3.31.

2. Cicero *For Milo* 92.

3. John Chrysostom *Homily* 30, 1 *Corinthians* 12:12–20.

4. Seneca *On Anger* 1.12; *Letters* 22.1; Pliny the Elder *Natural Histories* 11.144; Aulus Gellius *Attic Nights* 12.5.13; Pliny the Younger *Panegyric* 33.

5. Seneca *On Anger* 3.11.2; Cicero *The Orator* 2.84.

6. Libanius *Letters* 199.9.

7. Silius Italicus *The Punic War* 16.303–456.

8. Suetonius *Claudius* 34.

9. Seneca *On Anger* 1.2.4.

10. Seneca *Letters* 30.8.

11. Cicero *Tusculan Disputations* 2.41.

12. Quintilian *Minor Declamations* 302.

13. Athenaus *Banquets of the Sophists* 4.153; cf. Strabo *Geography* 5.4.13.

14. Cicero *The Orator* 228.

15. Quintilian *Institutes of Oratory* 2.12.2.

16. Pliny the Elder *Natural Histories* 8.160.

17. Seneca *Letters* 7.2.

EPILOGUE: FIGHTING BACK

1. Origen *Against Celsus* 8.44.

2. The two partly contradictory accounts are in Suetonius *Claudius* 21 and Dio Cassius *Roman History* 60.33.

3. Symmachus *Letters* 2.46.

4. Plutarch *Moral Letters* 1099B.

5. *Corpus Incriptionum Latinarum* 6.10193.

6. Jerome *Against Jovianus* 2.8.

7. Augustine *On Psalms* 149.6.

8. Cyprian *To Donatus* 7.

9. Tertullian *On the Spectacles* 17 & 21.

10. Orosius *Against the Pagans* 7.21 and 7.4.

11. John Chrysostom *Homily 37 on Matthew 10:7–9*.

12. Jerome *Life of Hilarion* 20.

13. Theodoret *History of the Church* 5.26.

SUGGESTED FURTHER READING

Those wishing to read the original accounts of Commodus's reign should begin with the epitome of Dio Cassius's book 73 of his eighty-volume history of Rome, then move on to the less reliable "Life of Commodus" in the *Lives of the Later Caesars*, and then to the third-century AD historian Herodian. It will become apparent that I have taken some poetic license as to the exact timing of some of these events, since Dio does not specify exactly at which games the rhino was killed, although it seems most likely that it was at the games of AD 192. I have also assumed that the games would have followed the normal pattern of such events, with standard features such as the procession and the prefight feast. The games were a highly repetitive and formulaic event, although the minor variations that separated one show from the next were part of the fun.

The games, in particular the gladiatorial combats, have attracted considerable interest from scholars. The following guide will show how indebted I am to many of them for their research, which has mostly been of a particularly high standard. Perhaps the best place to start for those readers looking to dig deeper into the phenomenon is the excellent sourcebook of translated primary material relating to Roman spectacles by Alison Futrell, *The Roman Games: A Sourcebook* (Oxford: Blackwell, 2006). This offers a wide variety of interesting texts with informed and illuminating commentary. Also Keith Hopkins and Mary Beard, *The Colosseum* (London: Profile, 2005) analyzes the arena games of the Colosseum in a stimulating and accessible format.

Those interested in the reign of Commodus should look at the attempts to rehabilitate the emperor by Oliver Hekster, *Commodus: An Emperor at the Crossroads* (Amsterdam: J. C. Gieben, 2002), and, if possible, John Traupman, "The Life and Reign of Commodus" (Princeton University Ph.D. diss., 1956). Also the article by Barry Baldwin, "Commodus the Good Poet and Good Emperor," *Gymnasium* 87 (1990), 224–31.

For Commodus's treatment of Christians, see Hippolytus *Refutation of All Heresies* 9.2. For epigraphical examples of Commodus's new calendar, see *Corpus Inscriptionum Latinarum* 6.30967 and 14.5291. The list of other emperors who either practiced or fought privately as gladiators includes Caligula, Titus, Hadrian, Lucius Verus, Didius Julianus, Caracalla, and Geta. See T. Wiedemann, *Emperors and Gladiators* (London: Routledge, 1992), pp. 110–11.

A readable and balanced overview of the spectacles as a whole can be found in David Potter, "Entertainers in the Roman Empire," in D. S. Potter and D. J. Mattingly, *Life, Death, and Entertainment in the Roman Empire*, 2nd ed. (Ann Arbor: University of Michigan Press, 2010). Ludwig Friedländer's *Roman Life and Manners under the Early Empire*, authorized translation of the seventh enlarged and revised edition of the *Sittengeschichte Roms* (London: Routledge, 1908–13) is still a remarkable overview of the literary evidence, and a very good read. It has largely been superseded, as has Roland Auguet, *Cruelty and Civilization: the Roman Games* (London: Allen & Unwin, 1972). Mary Beard, *Pompeii: The Life of a Roman Town* (London: Profile, 2008), has a useful chapter on the spectacles: "Fun and Games."

On gladiators, the range of books is vast but David Bomgardner, *The Story of the Roman Amphitheatre* (London: Routledge, 2000), and Thomas Wiedemann, *Emperors and Gladiators* (London: Routledge, 1992), are both excellent. Michael Grant, *Gladiators* (London: Weidenfeld & Nicolson, 1967), is still highly readable but is out of date. Of the many others on offer, I have found the following particularly helpful: Alison Futrell, *Blood in the Arena: The Spectacle of Roman Power* (Austin: University of Texas Press, 2000); Paul Plass, *The Game of Death in Ancient Rome: Arena Sport and Political Suicide* (Madison: University of Wisconsin Press, 1999); Fik Meijer, *The Gladiators: History's Most Deadly Sport*, trans. Liz Waters (London: Souvenir, 2004); and Roger Dunkle, *Gladiators: Violence and Spectacle in Ancient Rome* (Harlow: Pearson/Longman, 2008). On the film *Gladiator*, see Martin Winkler (ed.), *Gladiator: Film and History* (Oxford: Blackwell, 2004). Calculations regarding the numbers of gladiators and their likely mortality rates can be found in Hopkins and Beard, *The Colosseum*, pp. 91–94.

On more archaeological aspects of the amphitheaters, see Katherine Welch, *The Roman Amphitheatre: From Its Origins to the Colosseum* (Cambridge: Cambridge University Press, 2007); Tony Wilmott (ed.), *Roman Amphitheatres and Spectacula: A 21st-century Perspective*, Papers from an International Conference Held at Chester (Oxford: Archaeo Press 2009); and Charlotte Roueché, *Performers and Partisans at Aphrodisias in the Roman and Late Roman Periods: A Study Based on Inscriptions from the Current Excavations at Aphrodisias in Caria,*

Society for the Promotion of Roman Studies, 1993. On graffiti relating to gladiators, see Jennifer Baird and Claire Taylor (eds.), *Ancient Graffiti in Context* (New York: Routledge, 2011). On the Magerius mosaic, see David Bomgardner, "The Magerius Mosaic: Putting on a Show in the Amphitheatre," *Current World Archaeology* 3 (2007), 12–21. Analysis of the injuries suffered by the gladiators in the cemetery at Ephesus can be found in K. Grossschmidt and F. Kanz, "Head Injuries of Roman Gladiators," *Forensic Science International* 160 (2006), 207–16.

Clear and accessible introductions to and analysis of the Circus can be found in John Humphrey, *Roman Circuses: Arenas for Chariot Racing* (London: Batsford, 1986), and on the horses in more detail in Ann Hyland, *Equus: The Horse in the Roman World* (London: Batsford, 1990). On the importance of the Circus in the later Roman Empire, see Alan Cameron's two fine books, *Circus Factions: Blues and Greens at Rome and Byzantium* (Oxford: Clarendon, 1976) and *Porphyrius the Charioteer* (Oxford: Clarendon, 1973).

Introductions to the Roman theater can be found in Richard Beacham, *The Roman Theatre and Its Audience* (London: Routledge, 1991); William Slater (ed.), *Roman Theater and Society* (Ann Arbor: University of Michigan Press, 1996); and William Beare, *The Roman Stage: A Short History of Latin Drama in the Time of the Republic* (London: Methuen, 1964). On some of the public disturbances associated with the stage, see William Slater, "Pantomime Riots," *Classical Antiquity* 13 (1994), 120–44. On the staging of sea battles, see Gérald Cariou, *La naumachie: morituri te salutant* (Paris: Presses de l'Université Paris-Sorbonne, 2009).

Those interested in the psychology of the gladiatorial combats should see Carlin Barton, *The Sorrows of the Ancient Romans: The Gladiator and the Monster* (Princeton: Princeton University Press, 1993), and "Murderous Games," the first chapter of Keith Hopkins, *Death and Renewal* (Cambridge: Cambridge University Press, 1983), pp. 1–30. Above all, they should consult the excellent Garrett Fagan, *The Lure of the Arena: Social Psychology and the Crowd at the Roman Games* (Cambridge: Cambridge University Press, 2011), which also contains much interesting analysis of the games from a social-psychological perspective.

On the notion of leisure and how this relates to the games, see Jerry Toner, *Leisure and Ancient Rome* (Cambridge: Polity, 1995). On the relationship between popular culture and the games, see Jerry Toner, *Popular Culture in Ancient Rome* (Cambridge: Polity, 2009), where there is also a discussion of the sensory impact of the spectacles and the social and political use to which this was put.

On the games as a place of dialogue between the emperor and his people, see Zvi Yavetz, *Plebs and Princeps* (Oxford: Clarendon, 1969); Cameron, *Circus*

Factions, and Paul Veyne, *Bread and Circuses: Historical Sociology and Political Pluralism*, trans. B. Pearce (London: Penguin, 1992). Veyne contains the widest discussion of the concept of "euergetism," examining the reason why the Roman elite willingly spent such vast sums on providing the people with lavish entertainment. These works also look at the ways in which Roman historians use emperors' behavior as a way to understand their moral character. Rough calculations that a family of four received about 40 percent of the cost of their basic food requirements each year in state handouts can be found in Toner, *Popular Culture in Ancient Rome*, pp. 19–20. On the community focus of much of the social life of ordinary Romans, see J. B. Lott, *The Neighborhoods of Augustan Rome* (Cambridge: Cambridge University Press, 2004). On the importance of work in establishing identity and status within the local community, see S. R. Joshel, *Work, Identity, and Legal Status at Rome: A Study of the Occupational Inscriptions* (Norman: University of Oklahoma Press, 1992).

On the cultural messages of the games, see Toner, *Leisure and Ancient Rome*, and Magnus Wistrand, *Entertainment and Violence in Ancient Rome: The Attitudes of Roman Writers of the First Century A.D.* (Göteborg: Acta Universitatis Gothoburgensis, 1992). Also of use is Ray Laurence and Joanne Berry (eds.), *Cultural Identity in the Roman Empire* (London: Routledge, 1998).

Kathleen Coleman examined the dramatic staging of executions in her "Fatal Charades: Roman Executions Staged as Mythological Enactments," *Journal of Roman Studies* 80 (1990), 44–73. Donald Kyle shows how the confirmation of the social order symbolized by the ritual killing in the arena continued on into differential treatment of the corpses, in his *Spectacles of Death in Ancient Rome* (London: Routledge 1998). Both Kyle and Welch offer detailed discussion of the role of public executions within the games.

On violence and masculinity in Roman culture, see Erik Gunderson, *Staging Masculinity: The Rhetoric of Performance in the Roman World* (Ann Arbor: University of Michigan Press, 2000); and his "The Ideology of the Arena," *Classical Antiquity* 15 (1996), 113–51. On the use of violent images as domestic decoration, see Shelby Brown, "Death as Decoration: Scenes of the Arena on Roman Domestic Mosaics," in Amy Richlin (ed.), *Pornography and Representation in Greece and Rome* (Oxford: Oxford University Press, 1992), pp. 180–211.

On the Christians and the games, a very short introduction can be found in chapter 5 of Chris Kelly, *The Roman Empire: A Very Short Introduction* (Oxford: Oxford University Press, 2006). Wiedemann, *Emperors and Gladiators*, has a longer analysis.

INDEX